When the Handwriting on the Wall
Is in **Brown Crayon**

Discovery House Publishers

Books, music, and videos that feed the soul with the Word of God

Box 3566 Grand Rapids, MI 49501

When the Handwriting On the Wall
Is In **Brown Crayon**

Susan Lenzkes

ENCOURAGING DEVOTIONS

FOR BUSY HOMEMAKERS

Previously published in the USA in 1981 and 1985 and in Great Britain in 1988 and 1997.

Discovery House Publishers is affiliated with RBC Ministries, Grand Rapids, Michigan 49512.

Discovery House books are distributed to the trade exclusively by Barbour Publishing, Inc., Uhrichsville, Ohio 44683.

Scripture quotations are from the following versions of the Bible:
AV: Authorized King James Version of the Bible.
RSV: Revised Standard Version, copyright © 1946 and © 1952, 2nd ed. 1971, Division of Christian Education of the National Council of Churches of Christ in the United States of America.
GNB: Good News Bible, copyright © 1866, 1971, 1976, 1992 American Bible Society, published by the Bible Societies/Harper Collins.
TLB: The Living Bible, copyright © 1971, Tyndale House Publishers, USA.
Phillips: The New Testament in Modern English, translated by J. B. Phillips, copyright J. B. Phillips, copyright © 1960.

Library of Congress Cataloging-in-Publication Data

Lenzkes, Susan L.
        When the handwriting on the wall is in brown crayon : encouraging devotions for busy homemakers / by Susan Lenzkes.
                p. cm.
        Originally published: 1981.
        ISBN 1-57293-014-4
        1. Meditations. I. Title.
        BV4832.2 .L45 2000
        242--dc21   00-031543

00 01 02 03 04 05 06 07 / CHG / 10 9 8 7 6 5 4 3 2 1

Gratefully
dedicated to
Wilda Finefrock,
my dear Mom, now with our Lord,
who always encouraged me to write—
even though I started my career
on her clean walls.

And to
Herb,
now also with our Lord,
whose love and life gave me
the incredible gifts of

Cathy, Jeff, and Matt.
(I know you think you should get
royalties for your generosity in giving me
all this material to write about, kids,
but might this dedication cover the debt?
This one's for YOU!)

And especially to
our wonderful **Lord Jesus,**
whose grace was equal to my children's generosity,
leading us to joy and discovery in the midst.

*S*uddenly the fingers
of a human hand
appeared and wrote
on the plaster
of the wall.
(DANIEL 5:5, NIV)

Grateful acknowledgment is expressed to the following publishers for permission to quote the author's previously published works:

Tyndale House Publishers, Wheaton, Illinois, for the poems "Wasting the Present," "Discord," "High Expectations," and "Exercise in Love."

Christian Life Publications, Wheaton, Illinois, for the poems "Important Circles," and "Timely Appreciation."

When the Handwriting on the Wall
Is in **Brown Crayon**

*S*uddenly the fingers
of a human hand
appeared and wrote
on the plaster
of the wall.
(DANIEL 5:5, NIV)

CRAYON MESSAGES

When a message from God
would clear up confusion,
He could write on my wall —
or give the illusion.
But the writing that's there,
it's plain to be seen,
is a simple drawing
that I've yet to clean.

Lord, help me to learn
I won't be receiving
a miraculous sign
wrought through believing;
when each day I can see
and yet don't apply
Your messages looking me
straight in the eye.

I live in a home with three levels of fingerprints. Our house often has happy faces grinning from the bathroom mirrors and towels tossed about the floor. It's a house with bedrooms accustomed to popped balloons, banana skins, and dirty socks for decor — plus a treasure map drawn in brown crayon on the wall above the boys' beds.

My kitchen frequently seems to hold more used glasses then we ever owned, and the garbage disposal unit regularly gobbles dishcloths, scourers, and teaspoons. We sometimes refrigerate empty peanut butter and jam jars, and nobody ever knows who drank the last of the milk.

On occasion our home has broken dishes and broken bones, fear, squabbles, and tears. Other times it has hearty laughter and helping hands, surprises, accomplishments, and hugs.

And somehow, through it all, God has opened my eyes to His messages buried in each cluttered day: communiqués of love, words of wisdom, bulletins of understanding, signs of growth, and tokens of truth.

Such messages are as likely to be found in the erratic scribbling of the day when everything is going wrong, as in the flowing script of that occasional day that's going my way.

But that's what makes life as God's child so fascinating. I never know when I'm going to scrub crayon markings off the wall and find an underlying meaning.

Today, for instance, I finally got around to scrubbing that treasure map off the boys' wall. As I pushed my soapy sponge from X to X, I could see more than crayon marks disappearing. Each vanishing X seemed to represent one short year after another — all the time God has given us to map out His truths in the lives of our children — the time we're allotted to help them find the treasure of a vital relationship with Jesus.

Establish our priorities, Lord.

He who guards his mouth
preserves his life;
he who opens wide his lips
comes to ruin.
(PROVERBS 13:3, RSV)

THAT'S A MOUTHFUL!

Don't look now, Lord!
I don't want You
to see me
standing here with
my big foot
crammed in my mouth.

Don't worry, child.
If I didn't love you
just as much with your
foot in your mouth,
I'd hardly ever get a
chance to love you.

*M*others are often forced to utter things other people wouldn't even think. One day I actually heard myself yelling in my hands-on-hips tone of voice, "All right! Who put the fire engine in the toilet?" I'll always wonder if there was a door-to-door salesman about to ring my doorbell who forever imagines our bathroom with a garage-sized commode.

A lot of motherly queries seem to be preceded by the weary words, "Who put the . . ." and end with a scramble of objects so strange they could have been selected in a game of "I spy."

Over the years, anyone who happened to be in the wrong place at the right time could have heard me asking who put: the cereal behind the sofa? (the ants found it first); the pine cones in my handbag? (I discovered them during church); the lemon pudding-mix in the children's pool? (it was gelling in the corners); the toothpaste on the wall? (it looked like a fluoridated Picasso); the toy dish in the oven? (the flames were leaping out the vent); and the potato peelings down the drain? (the bathtub drain)!

Actually, parents should be taught not to ask questions, because either no one did it, or the other suspect did it. And if you ever do manage to pin the culprit, you tend to ask why. "*Why* did you put the rock in the refrigerator?" And then you get an answer: "Because I wanted a cold rock."

It's obvious that parenthood requires carloads of patience. And I could feel reasonably righteous about boisterously losing that patience when the going gets rough, if it weren't for the fact that God has to lavish so much of it on me.

Occasionally, after I've lost my temper with the children, I've heard my heavenly Father patiently asking, "Who put the foot in the mouth?"

*B*lessed are those
who hunger and thirst for righteousness,
for they shall be satisfied.
(MATTHEW 5:6, RSV)

*T*he soul of the sluggard
craves, and gets nothing,
while the soul of the diligent
is richly supplied.
(PROVERBS 13:4, RSV)

MALNOURISHED

Forgive us, Lord,
for snacking at Your feast,
nibbling at righteousness,
picking at Your promises,
and showing up at Your table
when we have time.

If we, Your own,
are undernourished by choice,
how can we expect to
feed a lost and hungry world?

*I*t's one of those hollow days — the kind that finds me tugging at the refrigerator door and then wondering why. When I look inside, nothing looks good, not last night's leftover roast beef, or even that marvelous imported cheese. Yet I am hungry for something. So I eat and find I'm not satisfied

Perhaps this means I'm starving spiritually. That must be it. I need to get alone and open my emptiness to God's fullness.

As I wait hungrily before the Lord on my knees, an interruption slowly opens the bedroom door. "Oh, no. Not one of my kids, Lord. Not now when I'm about to hear from You. Send him away, Jesus, so You can speak to me."

Quietly my little one stands beside me as I kneel, praying he'll leave, pretending I don't know. Silently he climbs onto my back, pounding me with his heartbeat, breathing softly into my hair."

Finally he whispers close to my ear, "Mommy."
"What?"
"Mommy, I'm hungry. Can I have something to eat?"
"Yes, sweetheart. I'm coming. It's almost dinner time."

And I rise from my knees, knowing my interruption is my answer, knowing God feels me clinging to Him as I wait to be filled — knowing it's almost dinner time.

*J*esus told his disciples:
"There was a rich man whose manager was accused
of wasting his possessions.
So he called him in and asked him,
'What is this I hear about you?
Give an account of your management,
because you cannot be
manager any longer.'"

(LUKE 16:1–2, NIV)

WASTING THE PRESENT

Forgive me, Father.
You gave me the
perfect gift of
right now,
and I threw it away
hoping for a
better gift
later.

*W*astepaper cans are usually no topic for discussion — unless it's whose turn it is to empty them. But this morning as I contemplated our bedroom wastebasket, trying to decide which child to blame for its unrelieved condition, I noticed its contents.

It was just the usual rubbish: cast-offs and remains, left-overs from our living. Wrappers and tissues, scrap paper and junk mail, cardboard tubes from inside toilet rolls and empty bottles that held shampoo and cosmetics, odds and ends, bits and pieces.

The ease of modern living creates a lot of refuse. And we're used to it. After all, there's always more where that came from. Some day the resources will run out, and the memory of our bloated wastebaskets will haunt us.

When my time on earth is running out, I wonder if the rubbish cans of my wasted moments will loom before me — minutes and hours casually discarded because there seemed to be an endless supply. I wonder who will be waiting to empty the wastebaskets then.

*S*o faith, hope, love abide,

these three;

but the greatest of these

is love.

(1 Corinthians 13:13, RSV)

PARENTHOOD

I searched —
but there definitely was not
a packet of instructions
attached to my children
when they arrived.
And none has since
come through my letter-box.
Lord, show me how
to be a good parent.
Teach me to
correct without crushing,
help without hanging on,
listen without laughing,
surround without smothering,
and love without limit —
the way You love me.

*T*hough I lecture and harp at my children and have not love, I will be background noise to rebellious thoughts. And though I wisely warn them not to use the street as a playground, or they'll be killed; and though I patiently explain why snails live in mobile homes, and I give endless answers to life's other mysteries; and though I have faith that can remove mountains of ignorance — yet never hug my children — I have taught nothing.

And though I slave over a steaming stove with balanced diets and complicated recipes and even burn my fingers — yet never smile as I serve — I have not really fed them.

A truly loving mother suffers through unfinished sentences, clutter, nicks on furniture, sleepless nights, and adolescent insults, and is kind enough to think her kids are the greatest. A loving mother tries not to resent her children for being free like she used to be, and she doesn't brag about how she never talked to *her* mom that way.

Real love considers a childish nightmare more urgent than her need for sleep; is not shattered by the title "Meanest Mom"; doesn't embarrass a toddler who breaks potty training or a teenager who still spills milk; steadfastly refuses to entertain visions of escape; and does not smirk as her child trips over the toy he refused to put away (but with silent wisdom rejoices in the effective lessons of experience).

Mother-love has arms strong from lifting, a heart large with believing, a mind stretched with hoping, shoulders soft with enduring, and knees bent with committing.

True mother-love never fails to point her child to the Author of Love.

*I*f it seem slow,

  wait for it;

it will surely come,

  it will not delay.

(HABAKKUK 2:3, RSV)

PACING

When I have to wait, God,
or when You want me to move
slowly,
I don't like it.
I don't know which is worse,
staying in my shell
or coming out and
crawling at a snail's pace.
Make me content to do
whatever seems good to You, Lord.
Your pace spells peace.

*W*aiting to see the doctor is not my favorite way to spend a sunny spring morning. But that's exactly how I spent this one. It helped, though, that there was a sunny-faced little boy to watch. This blond, wide-eyed young child completely captivated me and everyone else with his eagerness to experience everything a doctor's waiting room could possibly offer.

He checked out the chairs and their occupants. He covered his baby sister with her pink blanket and tenderly explained that there was no need to be afraid. He marched down the corridor to explore the toilets, and a roomful of weary patients' eyes lit with amusement as his giggle echoed from behind the door. Perhaps he'd discovered he was finally tall enough.

He strutted back down the corridor, arms swinging, and found a door that needed to be tested a few times. Magazines had to be straightened, and the holder for his sister's infant seat needed lowering. He carried on an effervescent conversation with a warm-hearted old man about the horror of injections and what it takes to be brave, his small round face registering complicated expressions with intensity.

Eventually, when he'd exhausted the room's possibilities, he announced with finality, "I'm tired of this place now. Let's go, Mommy."

"We have to wait, sweetheart," she said.

"But I'm ready to go. Let's get out of here!"

He didn't really understand that he was waiting there for a purpose, his good health. He'd been so busy exploring the waiting room that he began to think that was his purpose there. His inventive preoccupations finished, he felt he should move on.

Lord, sometimes *You* put me in Your waiting rooms. Help me to be patient with Your timetable. I need to learn all I can from those waiting rooms, but I should never forget that I must remain there until I see *You*. It's absolutely essential to my health.

*A*nd the ransomed
of the LORD shall return,
and come to Zion
with songs and everlasting joy
upon their heads:
they shall obtain joy and gladness,
and sorrow and sighing
shall flee away.
(ISAIAH 35:10, AV)

*S*ing to him a new song.
(PSALM 33:3, NIV)

DISCORD

God,
when there's not
harmony between us,
remind me that
You
are always on the
right note.

*D*iscouragement has landed. Vaguely I wonder why I'm discontent and feeling frustrated. After all, a Christian should be happy. I know, because 1 Thessalonians 5:16 says, simply and plainly, "Rejoice always." So a thick layer of guilt adds its weight to my discontent.

Sadly I sweep the same floor; wearily I wash the same dishes. And now I see it is time to repeat that familiar lecture. For here's my daughter, shaking her flute at me saying, "My teacher had better not give me this same song again. I'm sick of it! Seems like I've been playing it for the last hundred years!"

"My dear child, you're going to be on that song forever unless you learn to play it right. Stop trying to do it your way. Play it the way the composer wrote it, sounding each note correctly and surely. Then you'll begin to enjoy it. You'll be growing and learning — moving on to new lessons."

God poked me. "Listen to what you just said. Now give that lecture again, but to you from *Me*, the composer of your song. Play your song *My* way and you'll be happy again."

*B*lessed is the man
who trusts in the Lord,
whose trust is the Lord.

(Jeremiah 17:7, RSV)

*F*or thou art my hope, O Lord God:
thou art my trust from my youth.

(Psalm 71:5, AV)

TRUST

Stoop-shouldered, foot-dragging,
sighing resignation is not trust.

Real trust bounces on eager toes of
anticipation —
laughs with the pure delight
of knowing
in whom it believes —
rests easy
knowing on whom it waits.

Lord,
so wrap me in the
knowledge of You
that my trust is no longer
in You, but
is You.

*C*hildren are sweetest when no one's watching — or they think no one is.

I had just stepped into the kitchen with an armload of washing when the sight of our boys standing together on the back step caught my eye. Their backs were turned, so they didn't see me looking as the little one wrapped his arm around his brother's knees and tilted his blond head back, gazing up. He barely reached his brother's belt loops.

In a tiny voice he said, "Bend your ear down a minute — I want to tell you a secret."

Then, very quietly, he whispered something that delighted them both.

You know, Jesus, I can't help thinking as I watch them ... after all these years of walking with You, I still don't even stretch to Your knees. Bend *Your* ear down a minute, I want to tell You a secret. I think *You're* wonderful. And I really do trust *You*. When I grow up I want to be just like *You*.

*I*n just a little while
I will be gone from the world,
but I will still be
present with you.
For I will live again —
and you will too.
When I come back to life again,
you will know that I am in my Father,
and you in me, and I in you.

(JOHN 14:19–20, TLB)

THE TOUCH OF GOD

Jesus,
I long to see You
face to face.
But for now
I love the way You
smile at me through
the face of a sister,
touch me with the
hand of a child,
speak to me through
the voice of a brother,
are for me with the
heart of a friend.

I was at the drinking fountain, swallowing aspirin and complaining to my friend about my frequent headaches.

She turned, put her arms around me, gave me a kiss, and then simply said, "I love you."

Warm surprise told me I must have expected a sermonette on searching for causes, a dissertation on slowing down, a checklist of ten things for which to be thankful, or at the very least, "My, that's too bad," followed by a hasty exit.

I guess I always expect You to preach at me, too, Jesus. Oh, how I wish You were so real that You could put Your arms around me and dissolve my petty complaints with "I love you."

"My child, I can. I did. At the drinking fountain."

Today, Lord, You gave me love, wrapped in a warm hug. Maybe I can pass it on to somebody else with a headache, or a heartache.

*A*nd in praying
do not heap up empty phrases
as the Gentiles do;
for they think that
they will be heard
for their many words.
(MATTHEW 6:7, RSV)

SAYING SURRENDER

Lord, I've heard people say,
"Give God your wallet
and He'll have you."
You have my wallet, God.
That's easy —
it's usually empty anyway.
So how do I begin
to give myself completely?
"Give me your mouth, child.
It's never empty.
Then I'll have you!"

*S*ometimes I'm capable of impressing myself with my praying. Oh, not in public. *But certainly in private.*

The other morning I said, "Lord, help me to abide in the sunshine of *Your* love today, that I may radiate Your warmth to the world." Not only was God unimpressed with my words, *but* it rained all day.

Perhaps I should simply have said, "Lord, I never have trouble loving people when everything's going my way. Today will *You* help me to be willing to love when nobody seems to deserve it?"

I am learning to pray with the humility of true honesty. Yet even when I forget and start praying in lofty generalities, God pulls me up short by replying in specifics.

Not too long ago I blurted out, "Dear Jesus, I love *You*! More than pleasure, more than fame, more than approval, more than security, more than pride, even more than life!"

"More than pleasure?" He asked. "Then perhaps tonight you'll serve that extra piece of pie to someone else. More than fame? Maybe soon you'll write a great poem and forget to sign your name. *More than approval?* Then given another chance, you'll care more about your drop-in guests than your cluttered living room.

"More than security? Perhaps you'll trust *Me* for sufficient funds and still tithe. More than pride? Next time you'll fall flat and consider it a good position for prayer.

"More than life? I really loved you more than life."

*F*or the wages of sin is death,

but the free gift of God

is eternal life

in Christ Jesus our Lord.

(ROMANS 6:23, RSV)

DRINK YE ALL OF IT

Jesus, it was love
that forced Your trembling hand
to keep lifting, and Your
parched lips to keep drinking
the bitter cup of our salvation.
This was no toast to our health.
You raised the cup alone in a dark garden,
sweating blood,
crying out for some other way —
yet obediently tilting it
higher, swallowing acid sin in
agonizing gulps.
You drank for Your friends asleep nearby
and for Your enemies
converging with angry swords and a cross.
You drank for us all and drained the cup dry —
a pledge to eternal life.
I will remember, Lord. Eternally.

*I*t's spring and time to paint the house. I knew it was hopeless to ask, but I asked anyway. "Please, darling, could we just leave the ivy twining so beautifully over the trellis porch? It would be easier for you. You wouldn't have to paint that part. After all, no one would know except us. It's hidden."

But just as I thought, he insisted, "We'll rip it down — it must be done right."

I couldn't believe it. That ivy with its lovely profusion of green glossy leaves was hiding massive snarled twisted limbs — limbs that started with slender tentacles small enough to slide between supporting beams, had then slowly, insidiously, almost imperceptibly expanded, wrenching our house apart at the seams!

I stood looking at the damage and suddenly knew what sin is like, seeming innocent, so small at first. But it grows, slowly, insidiously, leafed over with deceptive loveliness, until finally we're torn apart, destroyed.

No wonder it took such a drastic clean-up as Christ's death on the cross to prepare us for an eternity with God.

Thank You, Jesus, for the costly gift of salvation.

She watches carefully
all that goes on
throughout her household,
and is never lazy.
Her children stand
and bless her;
so does her husband.

(PROVERBS 31:27–28, TLB)

IMPORTANT CIRCLES

Lord, sometimes I resent
being like a clock
going round in circles
hour after hour,
all day long,
week after week,
doing the same thing.

Help me to remember how
everyone in this house
looks up to that clock
every few minutes
all day long,
week after week.

I remember the day I wrote my list of helpful hints for harassed mothers. It was the same day I considered calling a designer/contractor to see about having a new kitchen floor installed — one fashioned after those ashtrays that whirl clean when you press a button. Toys, spills, dirt, clutter, even kids — gone. At the touch of a button.

It was the day I soothingly calmed myself with the rationale that the more dishes I broke, the fewer there were to wash — the day I decided to tell everyone the real color of our carpet was mud brown, and the sun had simply faded the edges to avocado green.

It was that same day that I hit upon the genius of stuffing both my toddler's legs into one trouser leg so that he could no longer outrun me.

No question about it — motherhood does seem to be a thankless vortex some days. Yet I need to realize that mothers run in highly important circles. It's easier to understand that truth when I remember that God entrusted His only Son to the care of a mother.

*B*ut the fruit of the Spirit
is love, joy, peace,
patience, kindness, goodness,
faithfulness, gentleness, self-control;
against such there is no law ...
If we live by the Spirit,
let us also walk
by the Spirit.

(GALATIANS 5:22–23, 25, RSV)

HARVESTING

As I examine the
vine of my life,
checking the growth,
I'm forced to admit
that the
fruit of the Spirit
doesn't include
crab apples.

*T*his morning as I sat at the breakfast bar drinking coffee and staring through sleepy eyes, I noticed our son's fish crowding to my side of their bowl gaping back at me. Most of the fish stared with wide-eyed innocence, if not a downright friendly curiosity.

But there's one crabby fish in that bowl. Oh, he looks beautiful — a sleek smoke color with a stunning silver belly. It's on his face that the real fruit of his personality blooms.

His unblinking eyes swivel here and there, with a searching critical stare. And the black-ringed mouth between those glaring eyes not only turns petulantly down at the corners — it openly pouts. It constantly moves in a gripe, gripe, gripe motion. The other fish work their mouths, too, but somehow theirs seem a more gentle kissing motion.

I wonder who's observing me, the look in my eyes, and the shape of my mouth? I wonder if I kiss my world with God's love often enough?

*For God is not
a God of confusion
but of peace.*
(1 CORINTHIANS 14:33, RSV)

RIGHT ON

Right is right and wrong is wrong
except, of course, when
right seems wrong
and wrong seems right.
But that means right which seems wrong
was not right,
but wrong to begin with,
or else it is delusion and therefore
still right. And wrong that seems right
was not wrong, but right to begin with,
or else it is
rationalization and therefore still wrong.
So once you've determined
what is right and what is wrong,
right is indeed right and
wrong is indeed wrong.
Right?

Our youngest child's nursery teacher met me at her classroom door with one hand steering my boy and the other partially covering a smile. As our little student bolted outside she said with undisguised amusement, "I've just witnessed a four-year-old theological discussion. I'd say your son won — at least he was pretty sure of himself."

At my puzzled expression, she explained that my boy had firmly announced to his friend over the morning snack that "God *flowered* Jesus."

Not stopping to question the feasibility of such an unusual statement, his friend simply took the opposing viewpoint and loudly retorted that in no way did God do such a thing.

"Oh, yes He did. I know!" protested our scholar. "It says in the Bible that God arose Jesus!"

I wonder how often God smiles, or laughs out loud at our limited understanding of His great truths? I wonder how often we spread our misunderstanding between thick slices of rationalization and determination and force-feed it to others?

We can find peace in the knowledge that God knows, and some day so shall we.

*L*ook after each other

so that not one of you

will fail to find

God's best blessings.

Watch out that no bitterness

takes root among you,

for as it springs up

it causes deep trouble,

hurting many

in their spiritual lives.

(HEBREWS 12:15, TLB)

THE ANSWER IS ...

Dear God,
I have a problem.
It's me.

Dear Child,
I have an answer.
It's Me.

*B*luejeaned and barefoot, I stood watering the flowers we planted in the place the ivy used to grow — that ivy my husband tore down when he was painting last summer.

As I drenched the blossoms of bright yellow, crimson, and white, I noticed again those green sprouts of ivy breaking defiantly through the ground. They were unwanted weeds disturbing the flowers. I'd had to snap them off several times before, and now it needed to be done again. The suspicion grew that I was feeding a chronic problem.

I guess the trouble stems from the fact that we let just a couple of roots in the ground. They were so big and had twisted themselves, snakelike, beneath the cement of our house's foundation, making it seem impossible to remove them.

I wonder if that's why I keep sprouting problems? Perhaps I harbored just a couple of roots of sin beneath the foundation when I tore down my old life, surrendering to God and His new plans. Now they're growing and interfering with the budding plants. I think I need to call in a Professional.

You do whatever is necessary to fix things, Lord. After all, my life is Your garden.

Thou preparest a table
before me
in the presence of mine enemies.
(PSALM 23:5, AV)

ON THE RUN

You've
prepared a table for
me, Lord?
A full-course
sit-down meal?
How lovely!
You know I'd enjoy that
but right now I am
on the run.
So much to do and
so little time to do it!
I'll grab something later —
maybe at the little
drive-through down the road.

You do own the
franchise on all those
fast-food places ...
don't You, Lord?

*I*f someone slapped a discount price sticker on me today, it would somehow feel just right. It's one of those all-too-frequent days when I'm on everybody's resource shelf.

My husband needs a button on his shirt, help finding his keys, and dinner an hour early; the kids need an arbitrator, a chauffeur, a nurse, an in-house garbage collector, and their PE clothes washed immediately.

The PTA needs me at a meeting tonight, if I care about the quality of my children's education; the Heart Association needs a volunteer, if I have a heart; the polls need my vote, if I want to remain in a free country; my Sunday school class needs a social secretary, if I don't mind; my friend needs a babysitter, if I have time; my kitchen floor needs a mop, if I believe in the power of bacteria; and my Bible needs dusting, if I believe in the power of God.

Maybe I should just run through the twenty-third psalm, since I'm in such a rush. It's so familiar — it shouldn't take long.

One thing though, Lord. Why does it say You prepare a table for me "in the presence of my enemies"? I don't have any enemies ...

*A*nd she brought forth
her firstborn son,
and wrapped him in swaddling clothes,
and laid him in a manger;
because there was no room
for them in the inn.

(LUKE 2:7, AV)

CELEBRATING

What have we done to Your
birthday, Lord?
You came in the dark silence of
night, with softly muffled stable sounds.
We "remember" with
stereos on high volume,
jingling bells, and loud parties.
You came to us surrounded by brown —
animals, mud floor, straw, and
wooden manger.
We "remember" with
brilliant reds, greens and glittery tinsel.
With our sounds and colors of
celebration, do we truly
remember, or simply
refashion
and thus reduce the glory?

Glancing at the lighted plastic face of the Santa decoration, as I was about to pull the plug on him and drag myself to bed, I had the urge to flatten his jolly dimples with my fist. It's not jolly old St. Nick on Christmas Eve, making his famous round-the-world trip in twelve hours. It's tired old Mom on Christmas Eve feeling like she circled the world, and not remembering why.

Shopping. Baking. Decorating. Corresponding. Wrapping. Entertaining. I'd been so busy making things perfect that I'd made a perfect mess of things. I suspected as much when I heard myself saying, "No, you can't have a gingerbread man. You'll get crumbs on my clean floor!" And again when my daughter asked for advice on her gift list and got instead a tiresome list of my endless duties.

But I knew for sure I'd scrambled my life when my youngest called from the other room, "Mommy, are you going to be in a good mood on Christmas Day?"

There was an exhausted mother that first Christmas morning, too. She was weary, not from parties and shopping and baking and wrapping gifts, but from giving birth to the Son of God, the One who came to us in simplicity so that we could learn that glory doesn't need decorating, the One who came to bring us peace.

"Mommy?"

"Are you still awake? Merry Christmas, Mommy."

*A*nd God is able to provide you
with every blessing in abundance,
so that you may always
have enough of everything
and may provide in abundance
for every good work.

(2 Corinthians 9:8, rsv)

ACROSS THE OCEAN

The echoing sound of
hollow stomachs, empty souls,
barely reaches me.
I'm in an important church budget meeting.

The cry of
motherless babies, godless people,
scarcely moves me.
We're planning events for an exciting year.

The desperate scratching
of ragged fingernails on closed doors
hardly bothers me.
We have urgent matters to discuss.

How dare these people
try to disturb us.
Don't they care that we have to
redecorate the sanctuary
this year?

*T*he Missions Board was looking for a "hunger volunteer." I glanced down, decided it couldn't hurt, and agreed to the experiment. *It wouldn't harm me, I told myself, to feel for a couple of days the way half the world feels all the time. Maybe then I'd care more, pray more, give more.*

The first morning I skipped breakfast, cleaned the house, and felt great. I drank a glass of water and thought how we all eat more often than is really necessary. I skipped lunch and my peripheral vision picked up the refrigerator as I drank my water. After twenty hours, water truly lost its appeal. As spicy beef and onions simmered on the stove I said, "I think I'll have a big tall juicy glass of ... water."

Now when your body requests beef and you give it water, it retaliates with its gagging reflex. When your nose sniffs rolls baking and you say, "Tough, have a glass of water," it pays you back by being ten times keener than usual. As I wrote to take my mind off food, even my fat dictionary began to smell tasty!

By the next evening I was becoming aware that my nerves were raw with hunger. So I valiantly called forth extra reserves of patience and humor for a scene of emotional trauma with our teenager. Somehow, it took me three times longer than usual to break through the misunderstandings. And when our boys pulled their usual bedtime stalling routine, I felt I was simply being righteously firm, but my eight-year-old said, "You've never been this grumpy before, Mommy."

The next morning I awoke with a stomach ache and a headache. As I fried the kids' eggs and buttered their toast, I honestly didn't want any. But my shaking hands said, "Eat!" so I did. And the shaking stopped.

What the rest of the world would give for a chance to make hunger a choice. I thank God for the privilege of giving until it hurts — I discovered that it hurts less than hunger.

*N*ow the serpent was more crafty
than any of the wild animals
the LORD God had made.
He said to the woman,
"Did God really say,
'You must not eat from any tree in the garden?'"

(GENESIS 3:1, NIV)

INCHWORM

Inchworm, inchworm,
what are you measuring —
an inch worth of sin
to be had for the pleasuring?

Inchworm, inchworm,
do you not know —
an inch worth of sin
can do nothing but grow?

Inchworm, inchworm,
though you're updated —
I suspect the Old Serpent
and you are related.

*S*uddenly shrieks echoed from the garage of our new home. "Help, Dad! It's a snake — I think it's a rattlesnake! Help, I can't get out. The garage door's locked!"

Telling me to stay put (he could have saved the time, I wasn't about to move), my husband rushed to our daughter's rescue, unlocking the door, reassuring her that "there are no rattlesnakes in our area."

Freed, she bolted inside to the safety of her room while I waited, trusting the Lord and my brave husband — in that order, because I don't trust *snakes* at all.

"Did you kill it?" I asked as he stepped inside. "Was it a rattlesnake?"

"Nope, it was only a baby. I scooted it into a bag with a stick and gave it to the boys to show their friend across the street."

My eyes widened. "You gave them a *snake*? What if it really *is* a rattlesnake?"

"Come on now," he soothed. "Stop worrying. I didn't see any rattles. Anyway, it was just a baby."

I followed him into calmer conversational waters, until we heard a commotion outside. The father of our son's friend was standing in the middle of our cul-de-sac shouting at neighbors to stand back as he brought his shovel down repeatedly on the head of our boys' new "pet." One peek in the bag was all their experienced eyes had needed. Apparently the canyons grow not only sagebrush, but rattlesnakes, too.

"We didn't know," I muttered humbly to our neighbor as we huddled our children near us. "Fortunately it was only a baby."

"Oh, they're just as poisonous. Maybe worse," she said matter-of-factly. "They strike, but haven't learned to release, so they just keep pumping venom."

Is there a small sin less deadly than that little rattlesnake, Lord? Do I sometimes take sin's power lightly, forgetting that baby sins have for their father the Old Serpent?

SECOND BAPTIST CHURCH BOOKSTORE
6400 WOODWAY DRIVE
HOUSTON, TX 77057
713-365-2317

1	6379550108 48	
	BIBLE TAB-STANDARD-SILV	4.99
1	6890752325 65	
	HEAVENS LIBRARY	3.25
1	9781572930 148	
	WHEN THE HANDWRITING ON	8.99
	OVERRIDE Discount	-6.74
	Sub Total	10.49
	Sales Tax	.87
	Total Due	11.36
	VISA	11.36

Saved with Discounts & Coupons   6.74

Signature - LIM/WAYNA
_____

Visa ************3065
VITAL Approval # 02307D (Swiped)
VITAL Reference # 20982220198 4
This Transaction # 1134941
**** Reprint ****
APR 7, 2012 17:34   1 -   JC

THANK YOU!
GIVE THANKS TO THE LORD
FOR HE IS GOOD
PSALM 136:1

*F*ix your thoughts
on what is true
and good and right.
Think about things
that are pure and lovely,
and dwell on the fine, good things
in others. Think about
all you can praise God for
and be glad about.
(PHILIPPIANS 4:8, TLB)

SANDS OF TIME

Lord, these incidents were
really just small irritating
pebbles
on the sandy beach of
my life.
So why did I magnify them?
Why did I feed their
disruptive power till all the
sands of this precious
never-to-be-repeated day
were shifted and stirred into
turmoil?
Jesus, I need the
balance of Your perspective.
Help me to magnify
only what's good and true.

Since all my days are Yours, Lord, even today belonged to You. (How often I wanted to say, "You can have it!")

The sun blazed through the window, prying my eyes open so very early. (However, I suppose it could have been raining.) And there stood my little boy with soggy pants and a cereal bowl. (Even so, he was smiling.)

The children dumped sticky cereal all over the shiny waxed floor. (At least we have enough to spill.) Phone calls and drop-in visits interrupted me at every turn. (Yet You have blessed me with friends.)

There was fighting, teasing, and screaming the minute the schoolbooks hit the table. (Still, my boisterous children are normal and so healthy.) Then my little one pulled all the buds off the only plant I ever got to grow. (However, You will make it bloom again.)

Now they're all sweetly asleep, Lord, and it's so wonderfully quiet. (Why didn't I remember all those "however" blessings while they were *awake?*)

*F*or by the grace given me
I say to every one of you:
Do not think of yourself
more highly than you ought,
but rather think of yourself
with sober judgment,
in accordance with
the measure of faith
God has given you ...
Do not be conceited.
(ROMANS 12:3, 16, NIV)

SELF-ESTEEM

Jesus,
teach me to
love myself
without a
megaphone.

Other women may not have this problem, but my mirror is positively unfriendly at 6 A.M. This morning I made the mistake of looking in that mirror without looking first in Jesus' face. As a result, I've been in trouble all day.

Over and over I've felt the need to prove that mirror wrong and re-establish my worth — to myself and others. Inadequacy has abrasively paraded as conceit. And no one was even watching — preoccupied as the world is with its own ego crises.

If I had spent time looking at and adoring God, I would have mirrored His love and moved beyond any need to impress. When I come to God, He accepts me with such completeness that I'm free to forget myself and concentrate on others.

It is only as I understand my worth in God's eyes that I can love myself in this healthy attitude of quiet humility and heart-felt gratitude. God measured my worth on the cross. There I cost Him the life of His only Son.

In the light of that cross I see self-acceptance as the responsibility to accept myself as God sees me — through Jesus Christ. I have absolutely no need for despair with such a God's-eye view. I certainly have no cause for pride, and positively no room for megaphones.

"I will praise the name of God with a song, and will magnify him with thanksgiving ... O magnify the LORD with me, and let us exalt his name together ... We love him, because he first loved us" (Psalms 69:30; 34:3; 1 John 4:19, AV).

Come unto me,
all ye that labour
and are heavy laden,
and I will give you rest.
(MATTHEW 11:28, AV)

MOMENTS OF QUIETNESS

The pastor prayed eloquently,
"Father, we thank You for moments of quietness."
Forgive my ignorance, Lord,
but what and when is quietness?

Oh, of course. It's the time the organ
plays softly and people cough
and babies fuss.
No? Then it's when I lock my bedroom
door so that children's squabbles are muffled
and distant.
No? It's probably when the dishwasher
finally stops and the television
blows a fuse.
No? Maybe it's when I sleep and only
the quiet noise of dreams scampers
across my mind.
No again? Then it must be when I'm
alone in the hills with only the chirp
of birds and rustle of wind.

"No, My child, it's when you are alone
with Me in the middle of life's
raucous insanity."

*E*veryone faces days when the idea of running away from it all moves from the realm of distant dream to distinct desire.

Given the choice, who wouldn't swap jangling phones for a silent meadow of daisies, or bickering kids for a permanent seat at the symphony? Who wouldn't exchange freeway fumes for cool salt air, or oceans of paperwork for rivers of hungry trout? Who would have trouble choosing between life's cramping frustration and open highways, or between conflicts and tranquil lagoons?

The trouble is, we're not often given such a choice. An even worse dilemma is to be given that choice and then find that there's no getting away from oneself.

It is bad to discover my own lousy attitude can foul up fresh air anywhere. It's discouraging to detect that my insecurities and nagging guilt can muddy the water of even the most remote stream of escape.

It seems there's only one real route to escape. Next time I feel like running away from it all, Lord, remind me to run to You.

*L*o, I am with you alway,

even unto the end

of the world.

(MATTHEW 28:20, AV)

BRIDGING THE GAP

Jesus,
meet me on the bridge
between Sunday's
aspirations
and Monday's
exasperations.

*L*ustily I sang with the recording, "... and I will never walk alone, for Jesus walks beside me." I stopped abruptly. Maybe it's not really true. Maybe it's just some lovely ethereal thought.

Surely, Jesus, I silently pleaded, You haven't sorted Your way through the piles of unwashed clothes cluttering the bedroom or tripped over the toys in the hall. Could You have sat with me on the edge of the bath cleaning sticky lemonade from the bottoms of Your feet, or gritted and ground Your way through that spilled sugar?

Did You walk with me to the medicine cabinet as I gulped a couple of aspirin for my headache? Were You beside me as I shoved aside newspapers and coloring books to collapse on the sofa for a minute, only to be roused by screams from the children as the day's tenth civil war broke out?

I know. You were there through all of it. It's not that I think You can't take it, Lord. Obviously, anyone who endured Calvary isn't going to be overcome by the clutter and tumult of family life.

Perhaps I'm just embarrassed to realize You've been watching me sink beneath the pettiness of it all — especially since I made such high resolves to be a better mother after I heard that sermon on Sunday.

It would help if I'd remember You're not observing, but offering help ... that You're the Rock above me, and still the Friend beside me.

I urge you to live a life
worthy of the calling
... and to put on the new self
created to be like God
in true righteousness and holiness.
(EPHESIANS 4:1, 24, NIV)

A SIMPLE STATEMENT

I know some, a few,
whose lives are a bold
exclamation mark! They drive hard in a slashing
downstroke towards a distant goal,
no larger than a dot.
Yet somehow they never connect.

And I know some, too many,
whose searching lives
are a question mark.
I find them wandering,
curving and sloping
towards that elusive answer.
They, too, never reach the goal.

But there are others, too few,
whose lives are a
simple statement.
They do not reach for the truth,
they live in it.
They know Jesus. Period.

One of my dearest friends is a talented choral director and a very busy lady. She packs twenty pounds of living and serving into every five-pound day. Her time is spent so wisely and purposefully that there never seems to be time left over for complaining or self-centeredness. She has no time for saying, "It can't be done," or "Nobody ever did it that way before"; no time to make room for small thinking and pettiness; no time to worry that someone might not like her.

Yet she is liked — no, loved — because she knows the priority of a vital, growing relationship with God, and the importance of sharing His love through hugs, smiles, and an occasional encouraging wink. She saves moments for love, laughter, and appreciation ... finds time to draw outsiders into her circle of warmth ... time to do a job better than anyone thought it could be done ... time to hear what's on your mind. And best of all, she spends a lifetime enthusiastically encouraging folk to be the best they can be for the Lord.

Once I slipped and fell in my walk up God's path. I was glad my friend called on the phone because I didn't want to look her in the eye. How easily she could have said, "I'm surprised," or "I'm disappointed." Instead she said, "I want you to know that I love you very much."

Not too long ago I sent her a card that said, "Knowing you has shown me so much of Him." That's a simple statement and a beautiful truth.

*T*hough I am
surrounded by troubles,
you will bring me
safely through them.

(PSALM 138:7, TLB)

GROWING

It's hard to miss those
boulders of trouble
that roll into my life.
They're big enough
to climb on, so
I take Your hand, Jesus,
and scramble up with Your help.
It's those pebbles of
pressure,
noise,
and everyday frustration
that are nearly stoning
me senseless.
Lord, toughen my hide and
soften my heart.
Teach me to walk that slow
winding cobblestone path to
Christian maturity.

*T*he morning greeted me with gray skies and a headache. The house was freezing. I shivered my way out to the kitchen to make the breakfast — no eggs, no juice, half a cup of milk. All three kids were at war, screaming, hitting each other and chattering non-stop. My husband explained that I was to go and buy a water pump for the broken washing machine sitting on stilts and leaking water in the middle of the kitchen. Then he left for work five minutes early without taking the kids to school. I shouldn't have blamed him — I wanted out, too.

Our teenage daughter was hysterical because her hair wouldn't curl right. Our youngest ran out the door in time to see Daddy's car rounding the corner and to throw himself screaming onto the ground. I dressed to the tune of further hysterics from the bathroom. Daughter had tried cutting her hair in a panic and "would rather be bald than go to school like this!"

Next we had a search for the eight-year-old's lunch. Then he went off to school without his medication. The car stalled ten times as I tried to catch him with that medicine. When I finally reached the school, I was handed a pink paper by a teacher carrying a sign. The paper said, "Please tell your child he has crossed a picket line. We are on strike."

I went home wondering whether it would be legal for a mother to go on strike. Absent-mindedly I began clearing up the debris. I tried to decide what to do with the load of dripping laundry from the broken washer. I removed the milk carton from the sofa and decided to leave the tools on the dryer and the old water pump on the TV. Wearily, I sat down with a cup of coffee and said, "Maybe I'll write something. How much damage can I do with the typewriter, Lord?" — just as the return carriage knocked my coffee all over the table.

Suddenly I was laughing. Only God would have known to pile just one more thing on top of my morning of harassment. I hope I laugh sooner next time.

*B*e still, and know
that I am God.
I am exalted
among the nations,
I am exalted in the earth!
(PSALM 46:10, RSV)

CIRCLES

I'm whirling in
circles
like a child at play.
As You spin by me,
Lord,
remind my dizzied mind
that I
am the one who is
turning.

*S*tanding alone in the dark solitude of the back garden, sipping hot chocolate and looking at the distant panorama of lights, I listened as the crickets sang with lusty, joyful abandon.

The sky was a blanket of blue-black with ridges of light clouds soaking up cast-off glow from an almost full moon — just dented a bit on one side.

I couldn't help looking at everything and saying as God did, "It is good." Only *my* voice had a touch of wonder in it, while *His* had only satisfaction.

So many days are spent chasing obligations in circles and nothing special seems to stand out as worth remembering. But five such unexpected minutes alone with God, just being still and truly seeing, truly appreciating, are worth a whole lifetime of chasing.

*He himself bore our sins
in his body on the tree,
so that we might die to sins
and live for righteousness;
by his wounds
you have been healed.*

(1 PETER 2:24, NIV)

GOD AVAILABLE

Almighty God
who made the
delicate field daisy and
the limitless reaches of space,
who made the babe to suck
and the soul to search,
thank You for being
God Available.
No, more even than available.
Thank You for seeking me
first — for searching along
the agonizing road to
Golgotha,
then finding me blindly supplying
nails for Your Son's hands.
And when
I finally found
You, Lord,
Your bleeding hand was
reaching for mine.

I started to call for her and then found her in the kitchen kneeling on wrinkled old knees in a circle of scattered rice. I watched, fascinated, puzzled, as she picked up a single grain and took it to the sink, washed and dried it, then placed it in a bag.

After four of five grains had been salvaged, I asked, concerned, whether things were really so bad that she couldn't afford to sweep up the mess and buy a new bag of rice.

"Of course, dear," she said. "I was about to do just that when I suddenly had a thought and put away the broom. If I do it this way, maybe I can understand God a little better."

At my arching eyebrows, she hurried on. "What I thought was, in all of God's tremendous universe there is a tiny planet called earth. And on this earth exists a creation of God's called people. We people broke loose from the perfect pattern God had for us and turned against our Creator. We really made a terrible mess of things," she waved her hand at the floor. "And sometimes I wonder why God didn't just sweep up the mess and start all over again. I really do wonder."

She shook her gray head, then took another piece of rice to the sink and began thoughtfully rinsing it. "Instead, He went to amazing trouble and pain — even to the death of His only Son — to salvage the original bag of people."

Holding her freshly cleansed piece of rice to the light she said, "... and the blood of Jesus Christ his Son cleanseth us — me — from all sin!" (1 John 1:7, AV). Then with shining eyes she placed the grain of rice gently in the bag as if it were worth all the world.

*B*ut our homeland
is in heaven,
with our Savior
the Lord Jesus Christ.
(PHILIPPIANS 3:20, TLB)

HINTS OF HEAVEN

Some day, Lord,
I'll be fit to enjoy
heaven's beauty.
But for now,
thank You for making me
human enough
to think true beauty is
mounded clouds snuggling a
mountain top,
water diving in a white frenzy
down a cliff,
palm fronds graciously
fanning Your skies,
delicate moss holding a rock
in its soft green clutch,
a child's corn-silk hair
flipping in the breeze,
fat baby fingers surveying
my face, and best of all,
that certain twinkle in
my husband's eyes.

Our three-year-old couldn't sleep. Creative thinking had conceived fear.

"Mommy, what will happen if the gas leaks and there's a big 'splosion?"

"There's no gas leaking, sweetheart. Don't worry."

"Yes, it will. Then what will happen to me?"

"I'm sure it's not going to happen. But if it did, you would probably be hurt."

"And die?"

"Maybe. But, Matthew, don't worry. Jesus takes very good care of us. He's with us all the time — you just can't see Him."

"He might die in the 'splosion then!"

"No, sweetheart. Jesus died once long ago — but He came back alive. And He'll never die again. He loves us very much. Anyway, Matt, when you die you get to go to heaven and see Jesus."

Great tears filled his eyes and voice. "Do I have to stay there? I want to come back home!"

My heart broke for him. Such frailty. Such need of me. Those fearful first steps of understanding what separation means. God, he's too young to call heaven his home.

Maybe I think I am, too.

Father, help me to set my feet, hands, and eyes on earthly things, but my heart on heavenly things. Today I need a touch of eternal perspective.

I will give to the LORD
the thanks due to
his righteousness.
(PSALM 7:17, RSV)

CEASELESS PRAISE

Make my praise for You
rhythmic, Lord.
No more capricious spasms
or irregularity
or discontinuity.
Move my praise in an
upbeat tempo —
pulsating, lilting,
vibrating, even swinging,
yet never ceasing.
Show me that
Your righteousness is
alive with
rhythm and song.

*I*t seems the bottom line on all our bills invariably reads, "Due and payable upon receipt." Who could miss it? We owe — they're collecting, and we had better pay up.

I wonder if God sends out such statements. I think He does. He tells me I owe Him my thanks, and it is due and payable now, not because my husband got an increase in pay this year, not because the kids escaped the chickenpox, not even because God used me to bless someone's life.

I owe my Savior constant praise and thanks simply because of His righteousness — His nature that is completely fair and just — His character that is total perfection and goodness.

This is good news. It means I can praise God when we don't get more money, and when all three kids are scratching at chickenpox, making scars. Even when I totally blew my opportunity to be a blessing to someone, I am to praise God, because it's *Him* I'm to praise — not my circumstances, good or bad — and not my performance, good or bad.

This is good news. Instead of feeding God a stack of problems, complaints, and requests at prayer time, I can enjoy a celebration of His righteousness. God has required of me a joyful, praising heart and has given me a perfect, unchanging Target.

*T*herefore the Lord waits
to be gracious to you;
therefore he exalts himself
to show mercy to you.

(ISAIAH 30:18, RSV)

WAITING LINE

I wait in long lines
wherever I go.
On the phone "please hold"
means ten minutes or so.
As I simmer at red lights,
my patience slow-leaks
For appointments I'm told,
"We're booked solid for weeks."
Yet the God of my life
stands in wait for my call —
when I need an appointment
there is no wait at all.

I didn't want to be late for this particular doctor's appointment because I'd had to wait nearly three months for it.

But the traffic was uncooperative and every signal in town was out to detain me. Red used to be my favorite color.

The next two hours I spent in the doctor's waiting room, watching people shuffle in and out of the corridor leading to the inner cubicles. You know — those little rooms that you always enter without a magazine because you ware naïve enough to think you were going in to see the doctor; those rooms where you entertain yourself by deciphering impressive pharmaceutical words on a line-up of antiseptic bottles; or try to decide why they don't have cotton on both ends of their swabs; or calculate just how long it will take an industrial strength air conditioner to freeze a human body clad in a flimsy paper gown.

When at last my name was called and the doctor finally came, he bustled in all smiles and apologies for the little emergency that had him running a "bit" late. And I found myself saying, "Oh, that's OK, no problem. Did you know that the squares on your ceiling have 194 holes each? Except for that row over there at the edge. You can see that those had to be trimmed so they only have 126 holes ..."

"Say, 'ah,' please."

I doubt that doctors really need people to say "ah" in order to see their throats. It might just be a good substitute for the sounds most people make when they're weary with waiting for the attention of a busy and important person.

It's hard to believe that the most important One in the universe is constantly available. I wonder if I tend to keep *Him* waiting just because I'm so used to having Him on call twenty-four hours a day?

Does he not
see my ways
and count my every step?
(JOB 31:4, NIV)

MOVING DAY

Here I stand, Lord,
waiting for the holy elevator
that will lift me swiftly, easily
to Christian maturity.
Make me content to take
one small growing step
after another,
climbing the stairs with You.

*A*pparently my celestial staircase was not built by the same construction crew that does cathedrals. In fact, I suspect it was thrown together by the crew that erects circus tents, whose motto is: Just as long as it hangs together till the show's over.

Today, for example, I climbed through a lot of clutter.

It was midnight when I finally got as far as the dirty dishes. They couldn't be done sooner because the peaches were rotting and it was either make haste and make jam, or make waste.

And the kids had been so bad all day, it would have saved time to set the alarm at ten-minute intervals for a lecture, a spanking, or a mop-up.

And the washing simply had to be done that day since our daughter had returned from camp with a sports bag of sopping clothes that were mildewing and required an accompanying nose-clip. Evidently they were caught in a downpour that nearly washed their tent away.

And there was the medicine I needed to pick up for the little one who had tonsillitis (again), but there was no one to watch the children until Daddy got home ... and he was three hours late, since they'd had another of their ritual emergencies at work.

And all this had to be worked in between phone calls from people wanting me to watch their kids for a little while, or work on a committee, or bake something, since I "don't work" and am home all day probably reading novels, watching soap operas, and painting my toenails!

It's difficult to remember that even on days like this, when my stairs are carpeted with problems, they're leading just as surely to heaven. As long as I keep climbing, keep laughing at myself, and keep looking up.

*T*he LORD delighteth in thee.

(ISAIAH 62:4, AV)

*D*elight thyself also
in the LORD;
and he shall give thee
the desires of thine heart.

(PSALM 37:4, AV)

DELIGHT FULL

I know You said it, Lord,
but I'm having trouble imagining
You delighting in me.
Patience and mercy
I can believe.
But delight?
You know that with me You get
intentions as often as accomplishment —
let down as often as love.
Delight?
In me?

Yes, child, I said it.
I delight not in your
excellence, but in your need of
Mine.
Delight!
In Me!

Now there's a command I can obey, Lord. How easy it is to enjoy *You*. As natural as a small child savoring a world that surprises with snowflakes on the nose; seeds floating on gossamer wings; tree branches that hold birds' nests, dancing leaves, and sweet fruit.

I delight — in Your love that reaches right through my wall of unworthiness; in Your holy perfection that causes my spirit to dance in worship; in Your power that somehow longs to be spent through me; in Your absolute worthiness that commends not only my delight, but my life.

Yes, Lord, I do delight in *You*. And You knew how it would turn out. I find that the desire of my heart is only for more of *You*.

How lovely that *You* arranged it so I would ask for the best Gift of all.

*H*ave you an arm
like God ...?
(JOB 40:9, RSV)

*N*either did their own arm save them;
but thy right hand, and thine arm,
and the light of thy countenance,
because thou hadst
a favour unto them.
(PSALM 44:3, AV)

OUCH!

Father,
why do I
strain my frail
wrists
when You offer Your
mighty arm?

*I*t wasn't until my compact car was trapped between the curb and the bumper of the car in front of me that I knew I'd been right. The parking space was too small.

Only one, positively no more than two miserable inches of space to maneuver that stubborn steering wheel — one exhausting inch forward, one weary inch back. Leaning back on the seat, I groaned at our decision that power steering was a luxury we didn't need.

It was then that he came, lightly touching the edge of his cowboy hat — a stranger with a smile, biceps, and a simple offer, "Let me help."

The smile had traces of amusement, mixed with sympathy. I didn't care. I quickly climbed out, relinquishing the driver's seat to this strong, capable solution. Let him wrestle with my predicament. He was better equipped to handle it.

Folding his six-foot frame into the small seat, he restarted the engine and in one stroke backed neatly alongside the curb. Open-mouthed with disbelief, I could only think, "Well, I knew I almost had it!"

Maybe, Lord, I'm always so tired because I lose my strength in the driver's seat struggling to extricate myself from my own traps. Then I lose the joy, finally hand it over to You, but saying as You solve it, "I knew I almost had it!"

*B*lessed be the L<small>ORD</small>!
For he has heard
the voice of my supplications.
The L<small>ORD</small> is my strength and my shield;
in him my heart trusts;
so I am helped,
and my heart exults,
and with my song I give thanks to him.
The L<small>ORD</small> is the strength
of his people.

(P<small>SALM</small> 28:6–8, RSV)

THE GIFT OF STRENGTH

Lord,
You tell me Your strength is a gift.
I'll accept that.
But I find myself holding out for
one huge package, wrapped, ribboned,
and presented with fanfare.
What did I do with all those simple
now-sized packages You
presented daily at
just the right time,
in just the right amount?
Is Your strength like manna —
plenty for now
but not to be stored?

I'm feeling weak today, Father, and totally inadequate for the climb before me. This job looms like a mountain. And I feel as though I'm climbing it, weighted down with an enormous backpack bulging with — what? Heavy responsibilities? The burden of my potential?

I've been struggling under the weight — scrambling over boulders, sliding on loose rock with frayed thin-soled tennis shoes, clutching at projections with bare and bleeding hands.

But this morning, when I finally stopped long enough to rest and lay my burden at Your feet, You opened that backpack for me. I was surprised to see it had a bow on it. Only presents have bows.

You showed me pitons and ropes, axes and hammers, and genuine climbing boots and gloves. I feel silly, Lord. Here I've been lugging on my back all the gear You provided for climbing.

Teach me to use all this equipment so that I can follow You all the way to the windy summit if necessary. I don't like heights, but I'll follow. Because I know and love the One who is leading, more than I know and love my insecurities.

*D*ear children,
let us not love
with words or tongue
but with actions and in truth.
(1 John 3:18, NIV)

LEARNING LOVE

God,
help me to love You
the way You
deserve
to be loved —
with doing,
not dreaming;
with obedience,
not oratories;
on my feet,
not just my knees.

*I*t's hard to say how many people could look at a picture of an old metal watering-can with corks plugging some, but never quite all the holes in its leaking sides and say, "That's me!" I said it.

The picture was on the front of a card my sister had sent me. "Never," I muttered to myself, "have I seen such a graphic picture of what keeps happening to my schedule. People just keep shooting it full of holes — and they're shooting faster than I can stop them."

I opened the card and read, "Keep plugging! Love you!" What a dear sister I have. And how reassuring to be loved with such appropriate understanding.

Then I noticed a postscript on the card. She had managed to turn her love into an action verb by adding, "Can I help you have some free time to write by borrowing your two handsome boys for a while?"

My sister definitely does not have time to love this actively. She has four active little children of her own, plus several more that she baby-sits. And since they live over a hundred miles away, when she gets our boys, it's for days — not hours.

Yet somewhere she must have learned the importance of loving not just in word, but in deed.

I'm trying to think of the last time I added a practical PS to my declarations of love to God ....

INSIDE JOB

The church was closed down, no worship afforded. Hearts were nailed shut before windows were boarded.
The sermon was vital, but really, it was dragging on a bit. Beside me a rotund man dropped his chins lower and lower, dozing deeply. Could I be hearing right — was he actually snoring?
He was.
In the silence of my mind I gingerly suggested, *It's* **Your** *house, Lord. Why don't* **You** *poke him?* and then watched. His leg began to move and his thumbs jerked, like a horse twitching at bothersome flies.

He slept on.

How could a person insult God by sleeping through a worship service? I fumed. *I wouldn't even consider napping in a church.*

Yet I had to wonder — do I excuse myself for drowsing through life? At times have I squirmed and shrugged, yet slumbered on, ignoring God's probing finger that called me to wake to urgent needs around me?

I wonder which is worse. Those who openly sleep? Or those who sing hymns and smile and tip God when the offering plate comes around, but are hibernating spiritually?

For you were called to freedom, brethren;
only do not use your freedom as an
opportunity for the flesh,
but through love be servants of one another.

(*GALATIANS 5:13, RSV*

BOUNDARIES

God, look at me!
Confined to pages flipped on the calendar,
stuck in a wear-dated body,
trapped in a tongue-tied heart,
bound on the ropes of repetition,
perimetered by fences of frustration,
caught thrashing in the net of humanity.
Oh, limitless Lord!
Give me wings to soar above the boundaries,
free in the boundless arms of Your love.

*T*he morning had been fairly routine — until I discovered the bird trapped in the family room. Someone had left the patio door open a mere sparrow's width, so one had hopped in.

Perched quivering on the arm of the sofa, the pathetic little bird splattered pale droplets of fear on the upholstery. At my startled sound, he took flight, crashing first into one window and then another. Finally, exhausted, he clutched a ledge for a brief and trembling rest before trying to break free again.

Soothingly, I spoke to him, "No, little bird, not that way. That clearly appears to be the way out, but you'll only break your neck. This way, see?" I offered, sliding the patio door wide open.

It's impossible to communicate with birds. I found I can't chirp their language, and my "soothing" voice only drove him back to bashing his beak against the invisible barrier that separated him from that blue sky.

So I hid and watched with silent frustration. He simply couldn't find the open door. Every time he saw white clouds through that window, he went once more for sure destruction.

Then a surprising thing happened. From outside, another sparrow hopped toward the open door. He moved right up to the side of the door, loudly chirping the way to freedom. And it worked.

As his trapped friend paused, he heard and cocked his feathered head, riveting his attention to the liberating wall. He jumped from the sofa arm, to the cushion, to the floor. He listened, not yet seeing, but following the call closer and closer. Then one more hop and he was out with his friend, flying free.

Sometimes I feel trapped. Sometimes I bash my head into life's unyielding windowpanes. It's at those times that I need to be reminded that You, Lord, are the only Way out. Thank You for brothers and sisters who care enough to sound the call to freedom in Christ

*A*gain Jesus said, "... do you truly love me?"

JOHN 21:16, NIV

EXERCISE IN LOVE

The best exercise for
strengthening our
relationship to God is
deep knee bends.
But why not in
a field of daisies?

*T*here's always someone who'll say it. Solemn with the weight of untold anniversaries, he nods and says, "Yes indeed. A good marriage doesn't just happen — it takes real work." He thereby places the maintenance of a healthy marriage in a category with push-ups in the army.

Marriage does require constant attention. And even the smoothest ones have an occasional rough spot. But if marriage is supposed to be work, I'd better start being nervous. Any minute somebody's going to catch me playing on the job, because when you really love someone, spending time with that person could be defined almost any way except work.

It's not drudgery, but a creative, exhilarating, and satisfying exercise in love. It's not boring calisthenics, but a lively game of tennis or a jog through the woods in springtime.

After more than nineteen years of marriage, I have not yet found myself saying, "Now I'm just going to have to make some time to sit down with my husband this evening and let him share what's on his mind." Those quiet times of sharing are cherished and anticipated. They're my dessert for a ten-course day.

God's Word tells us we are the Bride of Christ. Perhaps we can measure the health of that relationship by asking, "Do I spend time with Jesus from *eagerness*, or *obligation*?"

He heals the brokenhearted,
and binds up their wounds.
(PSALM 147:3, RSV)

REPAIR WORK

When a fractured leg is healed
it must walk again;
when a damaged zipper is mended
it must zip again;
when a sagging gate is fixed
it must swing again;
and when a broken heart is mended
it must give again.

*H*e came to me, large eyes wet with hurt and bewilderment. His hands, not quite four years old, curved beneath the cold stiffness of his beloved hamster. "Mommy! Jeff says Sammy's *dead*." A tear slipped, splashing on the soft white fur. "He won't wake up. See?" His finger gently poked at the unyielding side.

"Oh sweetheart, he *is* dead. I'm sorry."

"Why, Mommy? Why won't he move?"

"That's what 'dead' is, sweetheart. It means things don't move or breathe any more. It means Sammy can't wake up You see, he's not sleeping — he's dead."

He had asked "why" — why is there death? I had answered "what," giving a coldly accurate description of death. How can I explain the why of death when I don't understand it myself? Oh, I know that death is in the world because of sin. But why does a little boy's pet hamster have to die?

And why did our newborn baby have to die? All I could do was trust God for the reasons. I hoped in Him and leaned on Him. Still, that's not truly understanding. The cold fact is death separates. And death hurts.

How much more it must hurt those who don't have God to lean on, those who have no hope of eternal life in Christ Jesus.

I remember crying out, when the wounds of death were fresh and throbbing and my arms were awkward with their emptiness, "Dear God, what do I do with empty arms?"

Perhaps now I know, now that the wounds are healed.

Empty arms can reach out and hug hope into empty souls. Empty arms can embrace a sorrowing world that needs to meet its Savior.

Casting all your care upon him; for he careth for you.

(1 PETER 5:7, AV)

CASTING ON CHRIST

Lord,
how many times have I
gone fishing for Your help
with my pole of prayer?
I brace myself on the
edge of a sea of trouble and
with practiced style
cast my cares on You —
then skillfully
reel them in.
Over and over.
Maybe when my cares become
too heavy to
tie on the end of a line,
I'll finally lay aside
the rod and cast
myself
on You —
with no strings attached.

Our pastor had just implied that worry might be a sin. Then he leaned on the pulpit and said, "Will all those who ever worry please remain seated."

What an unfair approach! I was forced to remain seated and be labeled a "worrier," because if I stood, I was worried I'd be the only one. Plus, I felt a twinge of anxiety that someone might think I wasn't being completely honest if I got to my feet.

Being a very forward-thinking man, our pastor then taught us to worry scientifically. Evidently, statistics have proved that over 80 per cent of what we fret about never happens. So we waste a lot of valuable time.

To conserve this wasted time he suggested we make a weekly "worry list," jotting down all our concerns as they occur. However, we are not permitted to stew about these things until a designated time — say at three o'clock Thursday afternoon, if that's convenient.

If someone should happen to drop by and ask what we're doing, we're to say, "Can't you see? I'm worrying. I'm on number sixteen. I'll have finished in a few minutes."

Really, this is no joking matter. Some people struggle openly with this thorny problem. Worse, there are others who are well-established worriers and don't even seem to know it. I worry about these people most.

It's imperative that we recognize our propensity to label worry as "godly concern" and legitimize it as a recurring "prayer request." It's crucial that we acknowledge God's loving care and ability to handle these concerns. But it's most essential that we learn the freedom of casting all our cares on Christ, who is able to keep to the uttermost that which we *truly* commit to Him.

Then ... he said to them,
"Come with me by yourselves
to a quiet place
and get some rest."
(Mark 6:31, NIV)

HUG-HUNGRY

Often my hungry arms
ache
for a squeeze of my
little one.
But he's
digging tunnels,
tossing balls,
or running in the wind.
Much too busy for hugs.
Dear heavenly Father,
I seem so busy too.
Do Your arms ever
ache for me?

*W*hat's going on this morning, Lord? I have work to do. But the sun is coaxing me with bright promises and the day is blooming ripe with succulent choices.

It seems that even my household chores have turned on me, conspiring to tempt me with visions of escape. Rumpled sheets on unmade beds teasingly imitate tossing, swirling waves. Mounds of dirty clothes piled beside the washing machine emulate rolling hills waiting to be explored.

The shaggy green carpet, vacuumed, slyly suggests a sweeping lawn of vibrant grass, offering a spongy cool treat to feet imprisoned in leather.

I'm weakening, Lord! All this work will be here tomorrow — but will the son? Is wisdom sometimes found in following the heart to refreshment — in following the soul to You?

Maybe we should discuss this further with damp grass between my toes, Lord.

Maybe I need to rest in Your arms . . .

How I wish I were with you now
so that I could take a different
attitude towards you.
(GALATIANS 4:20, GNB)

NOW

Lord,
give me the sense to
love,
appreciate,
and spend precious time
with my children
now
so that some day
I won't feel the need to
smother my grandchildren
with attention
that belonged
to their parents.

One of my mother's delightful ideas is to write birthday letters to all six of her grown-up children. These messages warmly and lovingly assure us that we have, indeed, turned out all right.

My letter came today. Either it's terribly late for my last birthday, or a few months early for the next one — I'm not sure which. In either case I'm thrilled because she said she was glad I had arrived — glad I was born into her family, and doubly pleased that I was born again into God's family.

Musing on my childhood, she recalled that there was never really any friction between us, except in my tendency to be in a "dream world". She claimed I still have some of that in my make-up, but she now realizes this is the "creative" part of me. Imagine that! Just because I occasionally don't hear my kids talking to me when they're two urgent inches in front of my face, she says I'm in a dream world! She wrote:

I'm sure that you continue to find this creates problems and conflicts as you try to balance the practical everyday world with the ideas and dreams in your head and heart.

There are lifts to be given in the car, children's problems, husband's needs, minor and major crises, routine chores, and so on. Your ideas are circling around, putting meanings to all these things and your husband and kids are saying, "Look at me!"

It's a big job, isn't it? Putting practical on one side of the scale and just the right amount of creativity on the other to make a good balance.

Our time doesn't always have to be divided equally, but our attention needs to be concentrated wholly on one or the other during each encounter!

Amen to that bit of insight. All we have is now. And the now-moments with our children are as brief as a baby's first smile, as irretrievable as a missed hug.

> N
> ot by might,
> nor by power,
> but by my Spirit,
> says the LORD of hosts.
> *(ZECHARIAH 4:6, RSV)*

HIGH EXPECTATIONS

God expects
more than our best —
He expects
His best through us.

*I*t was only ten minutes until the worship service was to begin, and there was low-key panic in the choir room. We had been working hard, but the morning's anthem was a rough number. We were making it sound even rougher.

Of about seventy choir members that day, only two were tenors. The basses were lost somewhere in the first four measures and the sopranos were so flat that I kept looking to see if they'd been leveled by a steam-roller. We altos weren't so sure of our notes either, and our entrances and exits may as well have been unmarked intersections.

Our director wasn't wasting time telling us how we sounded, but was rehearsing us in a frantic double-time tempo — not even seeming to breathe between shouted commands. We all knew, though. We'd have had to be deaf not to know.

The last minute before we went in to face that poor unsuspecting congregation, our director closed her eyes and said, "Lord, we've done our best, and we need some help from You. Send Your angels to sing with us. We do this for Your glory." Then she told us to relax and enjoy praising God.

As we sang, it was all I could do not to crane my head to look down the rows of blue robes to see where those angels were standing. The expressions on the face of pastor and people mirrored our marvel. And they didn't even know that minutes before, our beautiful song of praise had been in musical disarray.

We may feel at times that God expects more than we can give. But if we ask, He gives more than we could ever expect. We are privileged to give it back to Him in praise and service.

*W*ho can discern his errors?
Forgive my hidden faults.
Keep your servant also from wilful sins;
may they not rule over me.
Then will I be blameless,
innocent of great transgression.
May the words of my mouth
and the meditation of my heart
be pleasing in your sight,
O LORD, my Rock and my Redeemer.
(PSALM 19:12–14, NIV)

SELF-PROTECTION

Protect me, Lord!
I don't mean just from
danger without,
but from danger within.
Protect me from
the folded pages of
self-deception,
the rounded corners of
convenience,
the glossy surface of
rationalization,
the wide margins of
broad-mindedness.
Protect me from
being pressed between the
pages of my own
willful ways.

*D*riving my son to school that spring morning I could see that it was one of those fickle days when surly gray clouds dare to mingle with the gentle whites amid startling patches of blue.

My concentration was interrupted by my young son's voice from the back seat, "Mom, the sun and clouds are taking turns." And I agreed with a laugh, as I removed my sunglasses once more in rhythm with the sun's recession.

But I knew — of course I really knew — that in God's nature the sun never recedes. That brilliant ball of fire never takes turns with anything. And the blue heaven is ever back there somewhere.

It's only the clouds that obscure — in nature, and men's souls. Black stormy clouds of trouble and sin, and white puffy clouds of selfish ease and lax attitudes come between us and the Son.

How prone we are to wander in the heavy haze of self-deception that dampens God's unalterable truths and waters down their impact on our lives.

Oh, for the wind of God's loving breath that scuttles clouds and haze before it, leaving clear the brilliant blue promise of hope in Christ.

*T*he things
which are impossible with men
are possible with God.
(LUKE 18:27, AV)

*B*ehold, I make all things new.
(REVELATION 21:5, AV)

CHANGE ME

Lord,
make of my hostility
hospitality,
of my brokenness
beauty,
of my pain
praise,
of myself
a servant.

It was lesson time, and father and eight-year-old son were hunched over a mathematics book.

"See if you can answer this one," I heard my husband saying. Was there a slight twinkle of playfulness in his voice? "Pretend I give you nine oranges and two eggs. How many do you have?"

Smugly and without hesitation, the answer came. "Eleven. That was easy. I'm good with numbers, you know."

"Eleven *what*, son?" The amusement was full blown now — Daddy had him trapped. He was about to demonstrate that you can't mix oranges and eggs.

I stepped into the study to watch the expression on my son's face. Pausing, with mouth open and brows thoughtfully drawn together, he said, "Orange Julius drinks, I guess!"

The expression worth watching was on my husband's face and on mine too. Had our son missed the point, or made it?

There are days I am expected to mix patience with problems and come up with peace. The equation doesn't always compute. I need to remember who the Miracle-Worker is.

Lord, help me to learn to hand You life's unmixables, then watch You add them up to something creative — something new, something called a miracle.

> No greater joy
> can I have than this,
> to hear that my children
> follow the truth.
>
> *(3 John 4, RSV)*

MY BOY

I look at the shiny-shaggy hair
and round, blue-gray eyes;
the small pink tongue struggling
impatiently against tiny white teeth
to form a word,
to convey an exciting newborn thought;
the broad little boy hand
covered with dirt, reaching
to touch my cheek;
and suddenly I realize
the astounding responsibilities
that are mine before that hand
expands to a man's hand.
O God,
hold my son's hand while he crosses
the danger-filled street to manhood.

*T*his was to be my stay-at-home-and-get-a-few-things-done day. That would be just fine, except for one thing: I have a toddler who wants to help.

I finish the washing, and he struggles with the piles of clean clothes toward the dressing-table drawers. I suppose a hundred years from now I won't care that they started the trip neatly folded.

I sweep the floor, and he insists on helping me by emptying the dustpan. In the overall scheme of things, I suppose the fact that he dumped the dirt back onto the floor is relatively unimportant.

I begin mixing the ingredients for bread rolls, and he insists on adding the flour. If I look at the situation optimistically, unbleached white is a good color on me.

I do know he's really trying, Lord. And I know he needs practice to learn. But it would truly be so much easier to simply do it myself.

I watch, filled with apprehension, as he teeters towards me, chubby hands cupping fragile eggs, and I'm suddenly aware that You, God, have entrusted me with the fragile life of this child. Guide me as I help my little helper become Your man.

*L*ive life ... with a due sense
of responsibility,
not as men [and women]
who do not know the meaning
and purpose of life
but as those who do.
Make the best use
of your time,
despite all the difficulties
of these days.

(*Ephesians 5:15–16, Phillips*)

TIMELY APPRECIATION

Jesus, please
teach me to appreciate
what I have
before time
forces me to appreciate
what I had.

Someone asked me what I'd change about my life if I could. I didn't like the question, because without pausing, my mind took one giant and well-traveled leap backwards to the church and the dear friends we'd left behind in the last year. My imagination nestled comfortably into the familiar memory of warm hugs, special times of sharing and prayer, and the relaxing comfort of knowing and being known.

I squirmed with the realization that I was being forced to choose between the past and the present. I knew better. The past is never a viable choice.

Yet had I been holding the present at arm's length in favor of warm memories? Was I building walls to insulate against future pain? After all, the relationships of today could become the losses of tomorrow. And just so, I realized, the lost moments of today would become the empty memories of tomorrow.

With God's help, I will not sacrifice any more precious clusters of days, or even minutes, to the fire of regret or the consuming backward look. For it is physically impossible to look backwards and forwards at the same time. And Jesus is always forward, calling us to keep pace with Him.

The LORD, your Redeemer
who made you, says,
All things were made by me;
I alone stretched out the heavens.
By myself I made the earth and
everything in it.
(ISAIAH 44:24, TLB)

HANDS OFF

When I come to God
with all my questions,
requests, and yes,
sometimes suggestions,
I forget with all these
needs so pressing
just who it is
I am addressing.
If God is God
He can act in love
with just my praise
and not my shove.
At last I see,
my heart understands,
why I'm taught to pray
with folded hands.

*M*y first clue that I'd been dangerously relegating God to the level of dusty sandals and flapping robes came this morning. I found myself handing Him a list of possible solutions along with my prayer requests.

Perhaps He doesn't need my help. I just remembered that all by Himself, without any assistance from me, He formed the worlds.

Scooping endless reaches of space, He moulded flaming balls of fire and hurled their shining light to the darkest corners. He shaped earthen globes and set them spinning about those fiery suns. Some He splashed with water and life.

He mounded dark hills, sprinkled their tops with powdered snow, and accented them with valleys of green — covered with graceful trees, gentle streams, and scampering wildlife. Reaching down, He punctuated the green with flowers of crimson, gold, purple, and white; then He set them all dancing with the sweet wind of His breath and sparkling with the light of His smile.

Forgive me, God, for trying to force You into cartons sized to my notions, needs, and desires. You cannot be boxed in. Forgive me for the ignorance of trying to mould You. Perfection is unbendable.

Mould *me*, Lord. Shape my mouth to fit Your praise, my feet to fit Your paths, my hands to fit Your tasks, my desires to fit Your will, and my understanding to fit the reality of You.

*M*y voice shalt thou hear
in the morning, O Lord;
in the morning will
I direct my prayer unto thee,
and will look up.

(*PSALM 5:3, AV*)

*B*ut lay up for yourselves
treasures in heaven,
where neither moth
nor rust doth corrupt,
and where thieves
do not break through nor steal.

(*MATTHEW 6:20, AV*)

TITHING TIME

Your Word says,
Give Me of your first fruits,
that which is new and fresh,
that which you'd like to keep.
Does that mean I must give You
the first hour of my day, Lord,
that choice hour for sleeping
or waking slowly?
Do You already claim that hour
for Yourself?
Have I been robbing You?
"You've been robbing
yourself, child."

*T*he news wasn't that noteworthy, even though we were watching the channel that continually sings its own praises, claiming lively and thorough coverage of the day's events. So I didn't really mind the interruption when it came. In fact, I welcomed it.

Our youngest son had plopped himself in my lap, slipped his arms around my neck, and then pressed his nose against mine. No chance of watching the news now — all I could see were eyeballs and eyelashes. He always has known how to capture my complete attention.

"Mommy," he whispered. "Could you get me that shiny bike we saw today? You know, the red one."

"No, sweetheart," I whispered back, going slightly cross-eyed with our close-range conference. "I'm sorry, but it costs too much money."

"Just write a check," he recommended.

Ah! So he had discovered checks — without discovering their principle. He didn't understand that we cannot withdraw what we did not deposit.

I do understand, but sometimes I forget that truth. When I try to make a withdrawal, needing reserves of love and patience, I occasionally find my heavenly account bankrupt. On such days it seems I'm trying to cash in to get the goods, when I've failed to set aside the riches of time spent with God and His Word.

No wonder Jesus said we are to lay up for ourselves treasures in heaven.

I'm glad He's open for deposits around the clock. I suspect He may have noticed . . . I didn't get my "banking" done this morning.

*A*nd our prayer
is for your perfection.
(2 CORINTHIANS 13:9, NIV)

*B*e perfect, therefore,
as your heavenly Father
is perfect.

(MATTHEW 5:48, NIV)

PERMANENT SOLUTION

My hair just won't hold a curl.
Every day it needs to be reset.
I guess I need a perm.

That's just like my goodness.
It doesn't last either.
Every day I run to You, Lord,
for more of Your goodness.

Do You give perms?
Oh! Eternity is permanent.

*I*t had become necessary to explain to my indignant son, not yet even a teenager, the difference between being perfect and being a mother. My explanation left much room for discussion.

As a very young boy he probably did think Mommy was perfect. Now that, in his maturity, he no longer lived under such a delusion, he'd taken it upon himself to firmly yank the rug out from under any false pretenses I might be standing on. "You think you're perfect, so we always have to do what you say. Well, you're not perfect!"

Bad enough to have to hear news like this — but from one so young! How soon today's children drop the blanket of innocence.

Actually, my son had simply and predictably ceased to equate authority with faultlessness. So it was time to explain perfection.

Perfect means without flaw. Perfect says, "No change needed." Perfect doesn't grow, because there's no place to go. Perfect just is. Perfect isn't a word. It's a name: God's.

Some day we will be perfect in Christ Jesus. In the meantime, we are in the process of being *made* perfect (see Colossians 1:28).

Perhaps our children are in the process of being made perfect through patience with us (see James 1:4).

NOTE TO THE READER

The publisher invites you to share your response to the message of this book by writing Discovery House Publishers, P. O. Box 3566, Grand Rapids, MI 49501, USA or by calling 1-800-653-8333. For information about other Discovery House publications, contact us at the same address and phone number. Find us on the Internet at http://www.dhp.org/ or send email to <books@dhp.org>.

OTHER TITLES BY THE AUTHOR

Everybody's Breaking Pieces Off of Me: Stress-Relieving Devotions for Women, © 1992 by Discovery House Publishers

When Life Takes What Matters: Devotions to Comfort You Through Crisis & Change, © 1993 by Discovery House Publishers

Crossing the Bridge between You and Me: Friendship-Building Devotions for Women, © 1994 by Discovery House Publishers

No Rain No Gain: Devotions to Guide You Through the Storms of Life, © 1995 by Discovery House Publishers, PO Box 3566, Grand Rapids Ml 49501, USA

GARCÍA MÁRQUEZ IN 90 MINUTES

García
Márquez
IN 90 MINUTES

Paul Strathern

IVAN R. DEE
CHICAGO

Library of Congress Cataloging-in-Publication Data:
Strathern, Paul, 1940–
 García Márquez in 90 minutes / Paul Strathern.
    p. cm. — (Great writers in 90 minutes)
 Includes bibliographical references and index.
 ISBN 1-56663-623-X (cloth : alk. paper) —
 ISBN 1-56663-622-1 (paper : alk. paper)
1. García Márquez, Gabriel, 1928– I. Title: García Márquez in
ninety minutes. II. Title.
PQ8180.17.A73Z936 2004
863'.64—dc22
                                              2004048614

Contents

GARCÍA MÁRQUEZ IN 90 MINUTES

Introduction

Gabriel García Márquez is a modern rarity, a
writer with aspirations to high art who also remains hugely popular. In this he harks back to
the tradition of Victor Hugo and Charles Dick-
ens. But it was not always so. There were long
early years of struggle during which García
Márquez lived in exile from his native Colombia, supporting himself largely by journalism.
By the age of thirty-nine he had published a
number of novels and short stories which had
gained him a growing literary reputation. Along
the way he had even picked up the Colombian
Esso Literary Prize. But none of this indicated
the storm that would break with the publication

in 1967 of *Cien años de soledad* (One Hundred Years of Solitude).

The publishers Editoria Sudamericana of Buenos Aires printed a first edition of eight thousand copies for distribution throughout Latin America—a respectable print run for an established literary author. To their astonishment, this sold out within a week, before it was even available in the bookshops. At newsstands and subway kiosks, *Cien años de soledad* was seemingly being snapped up by anyone who had ever read a book. From taxi drivers to nurses, from students to civil servants, people were immersing themselves in the fantastic history of García Márquez's imaginary city of Macondo and its founding family, the Buendias ("Good day"). Scientific inventions, the founding of a church, political uprisings, the arrival of the banana company, bastard sons being sent to Rome to become pope . . . this richly comic yet deeply poignant mélange of Latin American life was immediately recognizable to all who read it, from southernmost Chile to Mexico and beyond. It quickly became a best-seller throughout the continent, almost immediately achieving classic literary status as well. And this would be no passing phenomenon. Almost forty years later, *Cien años de soledad* continues to be bought and read, its Latin American sales now in the millions.

But this was more than just a Latin American event. Within years García Márquez's masterpiece was inspiring a similar wonder and self-recognition in readers throughout the world. *One Hundred Years of Solitude* would eventually appear in more than thirty languages, from Israeli to Indonesian, from Hindu to Hungarian. Wherever it went, García Márquez's book seemed to take on a strangely characteristic life of its own. Pirated editions appeared in Greek, Turkish, Urdu, and Arabic. The Soviet Union welcomed its liberated left-wing views but found it necessary to spare its readers the liberated sex scenes. In the United States the book's revelation of Latin American life and thought was welcomed, but the State Department found itself unable to welcome its author, declaring him a dangerous revolutionary and refusing him a visa.

Later the Colombian government decided to follow suit, issuing an order to withdraw his passport and restrict him from traveling outside the country. But Márquez was no longer living in Colombia and continued to travel the world on passports issued by other, more sympathetic governments. He resided in Barcelona and Mexico City, where he wrote further books, before being welcomed back to his homeland when the government changed.

Within two decades of its publication, *One Hundred Years of Solitude* had become the best-known Spanish book since *Don Quixote*. In 1982 Gabriel García Márquez was awarded the Nobel Prize for Literature, the committee announcing that here was an author for whom "each new work [is] an event of world importance." In their opinion his breadth of subject matter and literary excellence placed him alongside Balzac and Faulkner. Critics cited his ability to create a legendary world that combined both the fantastic and the realistic—though García Márquez, for his part, insisted that "every single line in all my books has a starting point in reality."

Meanwhile reality itself took on the garb of García Márquez's fantasies. By now Macondo had assumed an existence of its own, with several northern Colombian cities claiming to be the original of this legendary spot. Aging citizens in Aracataca, where García Márquez spent his childhood, claimed to remember several of the book's purely fictional events. A Hotel Maconda was built in the seaside town of Santa Marta (where García Márquez spent childhood holidays), while along the coast at Barranquilla (where García Márquez lived several formative years) a building was named Edificio Macondo and a local pharmacist's shop was called Farmacia Macondo. The public had long since taken Gabriel García Márquez to their hearts, calling him "Gabito" (meaning "little Gabriel"). Even the president of Colombia referred to him by his endearing nickname "Gabo."

On October 21, 1981, when the Nobel Prize was first announced, García Márquez was living in Mexico City. That morning all the pupils from a local primary school were assembled outside his window to sing a song in his praise,

11

and passing cars hooted him as he walked along the streets. In Colombia the headlines of the main Bogotá daily newspaper proclaimed "GABO NOBEL DE LITERATURA." When he set off on his journey to Stockholm to collect the prize, the presidents of a number of Latin American countries cabled their well-wishes to "Gabo," and he was accompanied by a Colombian band, whose music caused a storm in Sweden. The celebration party after Márquez's presentation proved a truly South American event, the likes of which had never before been seen in Scandinavia. The Colombian band played into the early hours, and the guests were further enlivened by the crates of Cuban rum dispatched by Fidel Castro under diplomatic immunity. Next day the Swedish government protested that the free consumption of so much rum was a violation of the country's strict liquor laws, and *The Times* of London ran a story under the heading "Castro's Rum Starts Anti-American Orgy."

In the most entertaining and illuminating speech ever delivered at the Nobel Prize ceremonies, Gabriel García Márquez opened by describing how "the Florentine navigator who accompanied Magellan on the first circumnavigation of the world, kept a meticulous log on his journey through our South American continent. . . . He related that he had seen . . . birds without feet . . . an animal with the head and ears of a mule, the body of a camel, the hooves of a deer and the neigh of a horse." The Florentine navigator went on to describe how, when they encountered their first Patagonian native, they held a mirror up to his face, and he was driven insane with fear at his own reflection. García Márquez continued: "This short and fascinating book, in which we can perceive the germs of our contemporary novels, is not, by any means, the most surprising testimony of our reality at that time." He went on to cite Eldorado, "the land of gold," which was featured on maps of South America for over a quarter of a millennium, its size and location changing in accord with the whim of each succeeding cartographer. Then there was the great expedition to northern Mexico in search of the Fountain of Eternal Youth, which lasted for eight years, in the course of which its six hundred members were reduced to eating one another until only five survived. García Márquez then told how during the colonial period "they used to sell in Cartagena de India chickens raised on alluvial soil in whose gizzards were found gold nuggets." This obsession with gold lasted into modern times, when the German engineers planning a railway across the Panama isthmus concluded that iron was too scarce in the region for the rails, so instead it would be best to use gold.

But gold was only part of the Latin American experience. García Márquez described how its rulers, in particular, created their own unique world. "General Antonio Lopez de Santana, thrice dictator of Mexico, had the right leg he lost in the so-called War of the Cakes buried with all funereal pomp." Then there was General García Moreno, who presided as absolute ruler of Ecuador for sixteen years, and even after he died "his dead body, dressed in full-dress uniform and his cuirass with its medals, sat in state upon the presidential throne." Serendipity and savagery coexisted in General Maximillian Hernández Martínez, the dictator of El Salvador. A firm be-

14

liever in the benign mysticism of Theosophy, he saw no anomaly in ordering the slaughter of thirty thousand peasants; he also invented a pendulum that detected whether his meals were poisoned; and as a preventive measure during a scarlet fever outbreak, he ordered all the streetlights to be draped with red paper. According to García Márquez, remnants of such history have persisted into modern times. The statue that proudly honors General Francisco Morazán in the main square of Tegucigalpa, in the Central American republic of Honduras, is in fact a statue of the Napoleonic Marshall Ney, which was purchased at a reduced rate from a storage yard of redundant statues in Paris.

García Márquez's tone darkened as he went on to evoke the contemporary history of Latin America, with its injustice, horrors, and bloodshed, of which Europe was at last becoming more aware. "We witness, on a forceful scale never seen before, the eruption of an awareness of the phantoms of Latin America, that great homeland of deluded men and historic women, whose infinite stubbornness is confused with legend." In an exasperation close to despair, he exclaimed: "We have never had a moment of serenity."

The history of the place, combined with its literature, lived beyond the record of the printed page, said Márquez, in every one of its inhabitants past and present. He spoke of the beggars and prophets, musicians and poets, soldiers and scoundrels of his native Colombia, "all we creatures of that disordered reality." Confronted with such a life, such a people had little need of imagination. What was lacking was the "conventional resources to make our life credible." This, he emphasized, was the solitude to which he alluded in the title of his most famous work. When judging Latin America, Europe applied its own schema, thus further alienating this people who were condemned to solitude. In doing so, Europeans preferred to forget "the life-giving madness of youth" that had once inspired their own culture. The pacifist Swiss, who now produced sweet cheeses and cuckoo clocks, had once been the most savage mercenaries in Europe, sacking the treasures of Renaissance Rome in an orgy of bloodletting. Returning to the present, he insisted that "those clear-sighted Europeans who struggle here for a wider homeland, more humane and just, could help us more if they were to revise fundamentally their way of seeing us."

García Márquez's Nobel Prize address was a plea for a proper understanding of his wayward continent, an understanding which would better be achieved by listening to the voice of its people. This voice had its place in the world; and in literature, as in life, it had not been easily achieved. The struggle to find itself, and make itself heard, had been long.

Latin American literature can be seen as the teeming unconscious of world literature: exotic when placed alongside the realism of the North American vision, prodigal and fecund in comparison with European literature, vivid and brash in comparison with Asian literature, though possessed of an almost decadent Latin sophistication which is eschewed by emergent African literature. It was never primitive, yet from its beginnings it was suffused with a fresh, often childish lyricism, which it would always retain.

Not surprisingly, the first great modern figure in this literature, who gave it a wholly characteristic voice of its own, was a poet. What is surprising is that this poet should have emerged from the troubled tropical obscurity of nineteenth-century Nicaragua in Central America, rather than from the more established salons of Buenos Aires in Argentina, whose wealth and economic development was already beginning to outstrip that of the "mother country" Spain. Earlier in the century, Latin America had broken free from its colonial masters, yet the cultural influence of Spain had persisted. Now, later in the century, this was beginning to wane, and the entire continent stood in need of a new and separate cultural identity of its own, one that would express its uniqueness and difference from both Europe and North America.

Rubén Darío was born in 1867 in Metapa (now renamed Darío, in his honor), a small town in the central Nicaraguan highlands. The country had gained independence fewer than thirty years earlier, and had only recently achieved an element of stability after ousting an adventurer from Tennessee who had declared himself president. Darío was an infant prodigy; by the age of fourteen he was already composing poems and legends that betrayed a bewilderingly colorful imagination. At the age of eighteen he set out on the travels that would last throughout the rest of his life. His first port of call was Chile, on the Pacific coast of South America. Here he wrote the first of many manifestos proclaiming the aims of an entirely new type of literature. Darío declared: "Words should paint the color of a sound, the aroma of a storm. . . ." Two years later, in 1888, he published *Azul* (Blue), his first book of poems and stories. This is generally recognized as the birth of the literary movement known as *modernismo* (initially, like so many such labels, a term of critical derision). *Modernismo* would sweep through Latin America and cross to Spain itself, purging the archaic literary Spanish of the period and transforming this historic language as never before. Instead of traditional long sentences, filled with modifying phrases and convoluted syntax, there emerged short, simple, vibrant sentences infused with vivid original imagery. Despite *modernismo*'s many adherents, Darío was always its leader and leading exponent:

> The cicada is singing
> its love for the sun
> whose gold-dust filters
> through the lacework of leaves.

Despite its fresh individuality, Darío's poetry remained heavily influenced by French Parnassian poetry, with its echoes of classical beauty. His exotic subject matter was interspersed with ancient mythology, and his descriptions referred to Paris or the Orient.

On his return to Central America, Darío's personal life was beset by tragedy and troubles. Within a few years his first wife died, and he began drinking heavily. This was the start of the alcoholism that would grow steadily worse over the years. He now embarked upon a second marriage with his former lover Rosario; but this quickly degenerated into a disaster of jealousy, infidelity, and final flight. (Rosario would attempt to track him to the end of his days.)

In 1893, in recognition of his poetic talents, Darío was appointed Nicaraguan consul in Buenos Aires. Amidst the cosmopolitan atmosphere of the Argentinian capital, his poetry became more detached from everyday reality, attaining a new, more troubled beauty. His understanding of the great French and Spanish poets of the past deepened, his mythical references took on a reality of their own:

> I seek a form my style has yet to discover,
> a bud of thought longing to open into a rose.
> Its premonition is a kiss placed on my lips
> in the armless embrace of the Venus de Milo.

In 1898 Darío traveled to Europe as foreign correspondent for *La Nacion*, a Buenos Aires newspaper. This was the year that the United States finally drove the Spanish from the last remnants of their American empire in Cuba and Puerto Rico. Darío understood that the threat to Latin America now lay from the power of the United

States. He addressed a poem to President Theodore Roosevelt:

> You are Alexander the Great and Nebuchad-
>   nezzar
> Taming wild horses and murdering tigers.
> You are a professor of energy
> so the clichés claim . . .
> When America trembles, we feel a deeper
>   shudder
> running down the long spine of the Andes.

Only in 1900, with the publication of *Cantos de Vida y Esperanza* (Songs of Life and Hope) did Darío's voice achieve its full maturity and relevance. Here the flowing melodies and exotic beauty of his work deepened. Objective description gave way to philosophical reflection and an awareness of the tragedy in the unpoetic real world that he sought to mirror in his determinedly poetic poetry.

> I wish to express my anguish in verses that tell
> how my youth of roses and dreams is gone
> that tell how my virgin life has been raped
> by an irresistible sorrow and many petty cares.

Yet he still retained the ability to celebrate—both his own feelings and public occasions—as in his often anthologized "Triumphal March":

> The parade is coming! The bright bugles can
>   already be heard.
> The sword-blades proclaim their presence
>   with slashes of light . . .
> the solemn glory of the banners
> held aloft in the hands of the heroic athletes.

Darío was not to know that this would become the favorite poem of many South American dictators. And it is under this guise that it makes its appearance in the works of García Márquez. In his novel *The Autumn of the Patriarch*, about a dying dictator in a nameless Latin American country, the poet Darío appears and recites his "Triumphal March." Whereupon the dictator remarks to himself: "This really is a parade, not like the shitty things these people organize for me." Here Márquez slyly contrasts the actual poet with the imaginary dictator. Both are mythical figures in Latin American history—but only one is real, only the ringing language of the poet continues to speak after he is gone.

Although Darío was only in his forties, his health now began to deteriorate. Not only his frame but also his spirit had become worn out with passion and self-indulgence:

> When the sexual rose opens
> all existence breathes
> its carnal perfume,
> its spiritual mystery.

During the long emptiness of insomniac alcoholic nights in anonymous hotel rooms he pondered:

> . . . a sad, nocturnal silence.
> Why does anxiety tremble in my soul?
> I hear the murmur of my blood,
> a soft storm unfolds through my brain. . . .
> The shutting of a door, someone walking away
> into the echoing distance. . . . The hour of the dead,
> when forgotten men emerge from their prison. . . .

24

> I pour this black wine into the glass of my
> sorrows. . . .
> The nagging weight of not being what I might
> have been,
> The loss of the kingdom that was intended
> for me.

On the outbreak of World War I, Darío left Europe; by now he was ill and all but penniless. In order to raise money he began a lecture tour of the United States, but collapsed with pneumonia in New York. He returned to Central America, where Rosario finally caught up with him. In 1916 some friends spirited him away to the highlands of his birth, where he died some months later from cirrhosis of the liver.

The journalism, the wanderings, the poverty—these features of Darío's life would play their roles in the lives of his great successors, none more so than in the life of García Márquez. He too would suffer a long journey before he discovered his own voice, with its unique blend of the personal and the public. But there was still more to be achieved, still more to be absorbed into the historic legacy that García Márquez would one day inherit and transform.

The next great modern figure of Latin American literature did come from Buenos Aires, the cultural epicenter of the continent. A man of universal learning, his life would nonetheless take on the form of some ancient primitive fable. The more he learned, the more his sight failed, until in the end he became totally blind, his vision confined to the world of his own mythical stories. Jorge Luis Borges was born in 1899 in the run-down suburb of Palermo, on the outskirts of Buenos Aires. He was descended from English stock and a family that included some military heroes of Argentina's history. His father was an intellectual who taught psychology in English at a local institute and had an extensive library of English books. His young son Jorge was a lonely child who grew up speaking English and Spanish at home. He soon began immersing himself in books from his father's library, entranced by the adventures of Robert Louis Stevenson and the scientific tales of H. G. Wells. The Borges family lived in a middle-class villa, but other parts of

Palermo contained dives that were notorious for knife fights and the tango (which in those days was bordello music).

When Jorge was fifteen, the Borges family set out on an extended visit to Europe, where Jorge finished his studies in Geneva. By now he already knew that he wanted to be a writer. In 1919 the family moved to Spain, which was in those days viewed somewhat patronizingly by Argentinians as the "old country." Comparatively, Argentina was rich, modern, and American—a land of the future. Nevertheless it was in Spain that the young Borges encountered modern literary Europe, in particular the Ultraist movement. The Ultraists called for a renewal of Spanish literature in a self-consciously brash, modernistic, "international" approach, incorporating such disparate elements as American jazz and French symbolism. At the age of twenty-one Borges returned to Argentina. Here, after his long absence, he was struck by the beauty and wildness of the city of his birth; at the same time he began enthusiastically introducing Ultraism to South America.

Although Ultraism was in fact very much an extension of Darío's new approach, it consciously rejected Darío's work as too abstract and outdated. Borges began writing his own poetry, publishing a collection of poems called *Fervor for Buenos Aires*. By now he was beginning to go blind. His need to wear glasses and his somewhat naive romanticism resulted in a number of unrequited love affairs. By 1930 he had rediscovered Palermo, with its gangster dives and vicious knife duels. He began writing his *Universal History of Infamy*, which consisted of short "fictions" briefly evoking the lives of a number of little-known lowlife characters, ranging from a mysterious eighth-century Turkic dyer to a twentieth-century New York gangster. Yet these minor characters on the fringes of history become, in Borges's telling, very much a part of the universal history of something far greater than themselves. For example, when a decidedly unlikely small-time con man arrives at the home of Lady Tichborne, claiming to be her long-lost son, for reasons unknown to him he is accepted by her—and thus enters "the tradition of classical tragedy." Such ambition, on behalf of the claimant and the author, becomes strangely plausible, when rendered in Borges's pared-down form and restrained style.

Then, at the age of thirty-eight, tragedy struck in Borges's own life. One day while running upstairs to the apartment where he now lived with his mother, apparently in the expectation of meeting a girl he had fallen in love with, "I felt something brush my scalp." The half-blind Borges had run into a glass window that had been opened into the staircase to let in cool air. The wound, and ensuing blood poisoning, brought him close to death. For several days he was unable to speak, and believed in his delirium that he had lost his reason. But when he recovered, it was as if the horror of his experience had freed his mind from the tyranny of its purely factual learning. He learned to rely upon his own esoteric tastes, following his quest for occult learning and quirks of scholarship. Now his fictions took on a truly original twist. Instead of dignifying essentially basic characters on the edges of history, he began evoking obscure fragments of history itself, bringing to them a curiously surreal reality. He was particularly drawn to historical tales of the mysterious and the unknown. In a lucid, matter-of-fact style, his short fictions began telling of another world more fabulous than normal reality, which somehow permeated this reality. His dead-pan style, filled with subtle references and ironies, managed to render the factual as marvelous, and the marvelous as factual: there were hints that pointed beyond the labyrinth of the reality in which we find ourselves trapped. Others, in other places and other times, had stumbled across enigmatic clues and achieved fleeting glimpses. Earlier adepts had set about hugely ambitious spiritual tasks, whose fragmentary effects lingered on. Here was a spiritual landscape rendered so as to be capable of encompassing all living history—and all reality.

These fictions might involve a magical object such as an aleph, or a dreamer who realizes that he exists only in the dream of someone else, or an imaginary planet, or kabbalistic symbols. Sometimes it is merely a shift in the way we perceive the world. In one fiction Borges tells of a man who remembers meeting a young Uruguayan farmhand called Funes, who had been thrown from his horse and left crippled. Afterward Funes found that he could remember every single thing and every single moment from his past. "I have more memories within myself alone than all men have ever had since the world began. . . . My memory, señor, is like a vast heap of garbage." He could recall every single leaf from all the trees he had ever seen. This continuous avalanche of memory made him realize how inadequate language was to convey what he was experiencing. Yet his mind remained so awash with memories that he could not impose order on his thoughts or form any abstract ideas.

In another Borges fiction the narrator tells of an obscure French symbolist poet called Pierre Menard who wants to write another *Don Quixote*. In pursuit of his dream he even learns Spanish, and strives to forget all the history that has taken place during the centuries since Cervantes wrote his book. He wishes to write the ultimate *Don Quixote*. In doing so he ends up by writing pages that coincided precisely, word for word, with the original. The narrator even goes so far as to suggest that these are in fact better than the original. Menard's style had not come easily, because he had not been Spanish and had not lived in the time of Cervantes. This made his writing distinctly archaic and affected for its time. The narrator carefully explains how this renders Menard's version more ambiguous and "infinitely richer."

Reading these stories, the young Gabriel García Márquez would begin to understand how to achieve the impossible. Here was a way in which even fantastic Latin American actuality—where the corpse of a dictator was able to rule from the throne after his death—could be turned into a convincing history of its own. Fantastic facts could be transformed into factual fantasy. The myths of Macondo, in its hundred years of solitude, could be made to tell the truth. Borges's elusive stories frequently made use of such devices as labyrinths and mirrors. Years later, García Márquez would be in the habit of saying that Macondo was "not real, it was all seen in a mirror."

Borges's one deep flaw, as a person more than as a writer, was his inability to come to terms with South American political reality. Yet he was able to remain aloof. During World War II he was dismissed from his post as a librarian by the demagogue Juan Perón, for his pro-English views. (Argentina was theoretically neutral, but Perón had fascist sympathies.) Borges was by temperament a conservative Englishman, an attitude that was simply inadequate to the vicious and volatile politics of the time and place in which he found himself living. The views he occasionally expressed were ill-advised and ill-informed. His sympathy for the "order and stability" imposed by the corrupt and murderous Argentinian military junta alienated many admirers both at home and abroad, and almost certainly cost him the Nobel Prize he so deserved. The fact is, he was childishly naive in political matters. García Márquez would be willing to overlook this in the author from whom he learned so much, but he could not forgive it of the man. From the outset, García Márquez was determined to become a Latin American writer whose work was relevant to his time, and this meant political engagement. His schooling in this sphere was learned from the third of his great modern Latin American predecessors, the Chilean poet Pablo Neruda, who was a lifelong Communist. As Neruda was fond of repeating: "You have to take sides in Chile. Either you are with the Cadillacs, or you support the people with no schooling and no shoes."

Pablo Neruda was born in 1904, the son of a railway worker. He grew up in Temuco, "the farthest outpost of Chilean life in the southern territories." In his *Memoirs* he described the main street: "Since the Indians can't read, the stores hang their eye-catching signs out on the streets: an enormous saw, a giant cooking pot, a Cyclopean padlock, a mammoth spoon. Farther along the street, shoe stores—a colossal boot." Within half a dozen lines he describes Temuco as "one of those towns that have no past" and one that "had a long bloody history behind it." This is at once indicative of Latin American history and Neruda's own enigmatic vision. (One is reminded of García Márquez's plea not to judge the continent and its inhabitants by the alien standards of Europe and North America.)

At the age of seventeen Neruda moved to Santiago, with the aim of studying to become a French teacher. Three years later he was lifted from obscure bohemian poverty and loneliness with the publication of *Twenty Poems of Love and a Song of Despair*, which proved an overnight success. It exhibited an unmistakably original vision: both casual and surreal, enigmatic yet at the same time frankly sensual:

> My kisses anchor, and moist desire nests
> in you with your arms of transparent stone.

Like Darío, Neruda would eventually find a niche in his country's diplomatic service. But it was now the 1930s, and the world was in the grip of the Great Depression; Neruda was appointed as Chilean consul to Burma, then Ceylon, then Indonesia—but these posts were without pay. In his isolation and poverty, Neruda found himself increasingly sympathizing with the teeming poor of the Asian street markets—descendants of a proud ancient culture ground down by colonial repression. Meanwhile his poetry descended into cryptic nightmare, expressing his own and a wider sorrow. The public and the private vision gradually became one in his *Residence on Earth*, though this vision remains both precise and at the same time elusive:

> When you run through the fields behind the
>   trains
> the lean ploughman turns his back on you,
> from your footsteps the gentle toads sprout,
>   trembling.

Further consular travels followed, but it was only later, when he had experienced the sufferings of the Spanish Civil War and an unsuccessful marriage, that his voice would become clearer, his poetic temperament more extrovert. In 1943 he returned to Chile and was elected a senator for a copper and nitrate mining region in the deserts of the far north, where "it hasn't rained for half a century." Here entire regions had been taken over by international companies, who ran them as their own private kingdoms.

According to Neruda, "They even imposed their own currency." He joined the Communist party but within a few years was forced into exile, fleeing in secret across the high passes of the Andes on horseback.

It was now that he published his *General Songs*, a vast epic which encompassed the natural and historical glories of Latin America, along with the anguish and suffering of its peoples. This reaches its peak in his celebration of Machu Picchu, the ancient Inca ruins high in the mists of the Andes:

> Cradle of lightning and humanity
> rocked in a wind of thorns.
> Mother of stone and sperm of condors.
> High reef of the human dawn.

Neruda would show that political writing need not be without lyricism and resonance, or "poetry." It could also be written for the simplest of people without sacrificing its authentic vitality—as he showed in his *Elemental Odes*, which included such simple paeans as "Ode to a Fallen

Chestnut," "Ode to Laziness," and the famous "Ode to the Tomato."

This celebration of a simplicity amenable to all would prove a vital lesson to García Márquez, as would the scope and pan-continental vision of *General Songs*, where politics and poetry became one. These latter two elements would also become inextricable in the poet's life. In 1970 the Chilean Communist party proposed Neruda as their presidential candidate, but rather than split the left-wing vote he preferred to withdraw so as to leave the way open for his friend Salvador Allende, who was duly elected as the Chilean president. Three years later Allende was toppled in a vicious and bloody military coup, covertly supported by the United States. Surrounded by tanks in his burning presidential palace, with military jets circling overhead, Allende committed suicide. Neruda died just twelve days later. In 1983, in his Nobel Prize address, García Márquez revealed how much all this meant to him, bitterly reminding the world of an outrage that many preferred to forget.

García Márquez's
Life and Works

Gabriel García Márquez was born in the small town of Aracataca in northern Colombia, a region of intense heat and fierce tropical rainstorms. According to García Márquez he was born in 1928, though his father insists that it was in 1927. Fewer than twenty years earlier, the American-owned United Fruit Company had laid out enormous banana plantations in the countryside all around Aracataca, and the town had undergone a spectacular boom. Champagne corks popped and naked women danced the *cumbia* before the banana magnates, who ostentatiously lit their cigars with banknotes. Fortune hunters, prostitutes, and immigrant workers from as far afield as Cuba and Venezuela were drawn to the town. García Márquez's grandmother would refer disparagingly to this deluge of drifters as the "leaf storm." In 1914 the town was struck by a plague of locusts, which many saw as God's vengeance upon the sinners. But within no time life was back to normal, with the dance halls and bordellos thriving as before.

By the time of García Márquez's birth, however, the boom had turned to bust, the population of Aracataca had been halved to around ten thousand, and the suffocatingly humid streets had sunk into silence. But the banana plantations remained, one of which was called Macondo. In 1928 the workers in the banana plantations of the Caribbean hinterland went on strike in protest over their pitiful conditions. This was brutally broken up by the army, who fired into the crowd killing a number of strikers at nearby Cienaga.

Gabriel García Márquez's father was illegitimate and a newcomer to Aracataca. He had been a medical student, but poverty had forced him to abandon his studies. At the time of the birth of his first son Gabriel, he was working as a tele-graph operator. In the course of his life he would father "fifteen or sixteen" other children, most of whom were illegitimate. Gabriel would be brought up among the extended family of his maternal grandfather, Colonel Nicolas Márquez, who lived the life of a provincial gentleman. He always wore a suit and tie, regardless of the heat and humidity. To the fascination of his young grandson, he kept a gold watch on a chain in his waistcoat pocket and believed in dousing himself in aromatic lotions. Although regarded as local gentry, Colonel Márquez was not originally from Aracataca. He was an exile from Riohacha, one hundred miles to the north on the Caribbean coast; here he had shot a man in a duel and had been forced to flee the vengeance of the dead man's family. In the army he had fought in the notorious civil war of 1899–1902, known as the War of a Thousand Days, during which around 100,000 people had died (nearly one in ten of the adult male population).

The two sides in the civil war had represented Colombia's two political parties: the Conservatives

and the Liberals. The Conservatives were supported by right-wing elements in the military, as
well as the church; they also incorporated various
fascist elements who believed in restricting the
vote. The Liberals stemmed from those in the military who had supported Simón Bolívar, the great
liberator of Latin America, also gaining wide-
spread support among the commercial class who
wished to restrict the power of the church, and
even from landowners whose estates needed local
military protection. Occasionally the Liberals
would throw up an authentic populist politician,
while out of the ranks of the Conservatives there
might emerge a leader of genuine political skill—
but for the most part both parties continued to be
ruled by their own upper-class factions, who
merely sought their own gain. The two parties
continued to rule the country, alternating in power,
depending upon who fixed the elections more
effectively.

Colonel Márquez was a leading member of
the Liberal party caucus that controlled Aracataca. Owing to his party allegiance, the Conservative government in Bogotá refused to send him

the army pension to which he was entitled. The young Gabriel García Márquez grew up in childish awe of his grandfather, in later life recalling him as "the biggest eater I can remember and the most outrageous fornicator." Despite the Colonel's outrage at his son-in-law's behavior, he too had over a dozen illegitimate children. It was the Colonel who one day took young Gabito to the local United Fruit Company stores and first showed him ice—an incident that is transformed into a miraculous scene at the opening of *One Hundred Years of Solitude*.

The household in which Gabito grew up also contained a number of unusual women; these too would appear in one form or another in his later works. His grandmother Tranquilina, who was blind, occupied a world of magical superstition. To the apprehensive fear of Gabito, she would talk of the dead and spirits from the underworld, who flitted in and out of her life with the same constancy as the living. Aunt Francisca sat weaving her own shroud, explaining to Gabito that she did this "because one day I am going to die." And when she had finished, she lay down and did just that. A certain room in the house always remained empty, and no one went into it, because this was where Aunt Petra had died.

When Gabito was eight, the Colonel became ill and died. Around this time Gabito went to live with his father, who had now become a pharmacist in the coastal town of Barranquilla. Here Gabito went to school at the local Jesuit college. He proved a promising pupil but felt lonely after the communal life in his grandfather's house. He spent his time reading Alexandre Dumas and Jules Verne, his mind only coming alive amidst the swashbuckling adventures of the Three Musketeers or on a journey twenty thousand leagues under the sea. At the age of thirteen he won a scholarship to the Liceo Nacional, a state-run boarding school for gifted children. This was at Zipaquirá, thirty miles north of the capital Bogotá. The five-hundred-mile journey took him over a week, involving a long steamer journey up the Magdalena River, followed by a slow, snaking train ride high into the Andes. This was a Colombia that Gabito had never seen before. After the vivid colors and smells of the steamy

44

north, this was a cool grey world. Even the people were different. The population of the tropical north was Caribbean, a volatile mix of African, South American Indian, and Spanish stock. In the interior, over eight thousand feet up in the high Andes, the inhabitants were still largely white: the descendants of Spanish colonials, with pale faces and mournful expressions.

García Márquez would later describe his arrival in Bogotá, "a remote and mournful city, where a cold drizzle had been falling since the beginning of the sixteenth century. I suffered its bitterness for the first time one ill-fated afternoon in January, the saddest in my life. . . . Bogotá was dismal, smelling of soot . . . and men dressed in black, with black hats, went stumbling through the streets. . . . You only saw a woman occasionally, since they were not allowed in the majority of public places." In his later fiction he would imagine how "on ghostly nights, the carriages of the viceroys still rattled through the narrow stone streets." In colonial times this had been the residence of the Spanish viceroy, with Bogotá ruling as the political and intellectual capital of New Granada, which occupied the whole of northern South America. By 1821 this region had been liberated by Simón Bolívar, becoming Gran Colombia. But within ten years this unwieldy country had simply fallen apart into Ecuador, Venezuela, and Colombia, leaving Bogotá the capital of a remnant nation of just four million people. There had followed over a century of almost continuous violence, to the point where the country's historian, J. L. Payne, would declare: "On a scale of political deaths per generation, Colombia has one of the highest levels of political conflict in the world." Some observers consider even this to be too modest an estimation. One of the rare moments of peace in the entire history of Colombia took place during the few years following the War of a Thousand Days, when it is generally reckoned that those who survived were simply too exhausted to continue with the struggle and needed a period of recuperation before they could launch into the next period of violence.

Gabo found the Liceo Nacional like "a convent with no heating and no flowers." The education was of a good standard, and he excelled in literature while doing poorly at science. Yet it was his leftist science teachers who later introduced him to socialism and the ideas of Marx. During the long, lonely weekends, Gabo would hide away in the library. By his last years at school, he had begun absorbing a heady mixture of Freud's *Interpretation of Dreams* and *The Prophecies of Nostradamus*. The headmaster was also something of a poet, and it was he who introduced Gabo to the works of Rubén Darío. Gabo felt an immediate affinity with Darío: they had both grown up in a remote provincial town in a minor Latin American country. Darío had shown that it was possible to rise from such a background to become a writer of world renown. Gabo's vague ideas began to crystallize: he decided that he too would become a famous writer.

But when he left the Liceo Nacional at the age of eighteen, this ambition was little more than a dream. On his arrival home his father persuaded him to pursue a "serious" career, and so in 1947 García Márquez entered the University of Bogotá to study law. He quickly became bored with his lectures and took to hanging around in the cafés. He grew a mustache, let his hair grow long, and began writing poetry. During the evenings he liked to drink rum and attend wild parties. In his student lodgings he had to share a room, but he soon found a way of escaping into the solitude which he now found so precious—where he could read and think and write poetry. He would buy a five-cent ticket for the tram that plied the circular route around the city, and for hours on end he would simply vanish. Here he first began reading Kafka, in an edition translated by Borges. This inspired him to write a short story called "The Third Resignation." In this "autobiographical parable" García Márquez described how a boy who had died at the age of seven remained alive for eighteen years in his coffin. The boy's mind was aware of sensations and memories, and he was capable of imagination, while his body gradually putrified. Shortly after this, a critic in the Bogotá daily *El Espectador* wrote an article describing the younger generation of Colombian writers as a talentless bunch, devoid of either originality or imagination. He ended by challenging any of them to prove him wrong. García Márquez decided to send in his short story. He was more than surprised when the following Sunday he happened to glance over the shoulder of someone reading *El Espectador* and saw his story in print. A note introducing the story announced that "with Gabriel García Márquez a new and notable writer has come into being."

During García Márquez's second year at university, political events came to a head. Jorge Eliecer Gaitan, the populist leader of the Liberal party, was shot dead on a street in Bogotá. This provoked a spontaneous riot, and as news of the assassination spread throughout the city, thousands took to the streets. Mobs began looting shops and setting fire to buildings. The militia fired tear gas in an attempt to clear the streets, then began shooting into the crowds. After the rioters seized the state-run radio station and began broadcasting their grievances, the violence spread throughout the country. When the *Bogotaza*, as the uprising became known, finally subsided after several days of anarchy, hundreds were left dead in the streets of the capital alone.

Colombia now embarked upon a prolonged period of civil instability during which as many as 300,000 died throughout the country. This period became known as *La Violencia* and lasted for the next *eighteen years*. (Ironically, the assassination that sparked this time of troubles was not the work of the Conservatives but of elements among the Liberal elite who wished to suppress Gaitan's populist—in other words, more genuinely liberal—views.)

García Márquez found himself caught up in the riots on the streets of Bogotá, during which he witnessed a mob setting fire to his student lodgings. He made an attempt to save his books and manuscripts from the blaze, but this proved futile. He was reduced to tears of frustration and despair as he watched his work burn. The *Bogotaza* would prove a turning point in his life. He realized that he had been blind to the circumstances of those living around him. Witnessing these events would transform him from a self-absorbed, somewhat private character into a man of political conviction who determinedly espoused the cause of the left.

In the aftermath of the *Bogotaza*, the University of Bogotá was shut down for the duration, cafés remained boarded up, and armed troops patrolled the streets of burnt-out buildings. García Márquez returned to his family home in the Caribbean region, which remained comparatively calm and stable while the events of *La Violencia* continued to sweep the country. In keeping with his father's wishes, García Márquez ostensibly continued his law studies at the University of Cartagena, but by now he had lost all interest in the subject. When a new Liberal paper called *El Universal* opened in Cartagena, he managed to persuade the editor to take him on as a journalist. This not only provided him with much-needed financial support but also gave him the chance to express his views. The editor had been so impressed by García Márquez that he gave him a daily five-hundred-word column of his own, announcng his new young columnist as a "scholar, writer and intellectual who will use his spirited imagination to express his reaction to people and events."

Yet when García Márquez began delivering his written columns, he was in for a shock. The editor was none too pleased with his undisciplined style and awkward literary flourishes. Long editorial sessions ensued, during which García Márquez watched his articles being taken apart sentence by sentence and rewritten in acceptable style. He was naturally irritated, but looking back on these sessions years later he would admit that it was here he learned many of the basic ingredients of writing. A style could be complex yet at the same time clear: the clarity lay in its comprehensibility. He also learned that journalism and literary writing did not necessarily have different subject matter. A fusion between literature and the accidental events of daily life was growing in his mind.

García Márquez would work at *El Universal* through the night. By dawn the paper was printed and ready for circulation. When the offices closed down, he would make for the nearby port, where he would drink rum in the run-down bars, listening to the stories of seamen and dockers. Many of these rum-inspired fantasies would reappear in his later writing, presented as wondrous factual events in Macondo and other locales.

Overwork and overdrinking eventually caught up with García Márquez, and he was struck down with pneumonia. He returned to the home of his mother and father, who now lived a hundred miles inland at the river port of Sucre. Here he recuperated from his illness, devouring stacks of books, especially modern American writers such as Faulkner and Hemingway. He became fascinated by the apparent simplicity of Hemingway's stories, whose transparent style left out all irrelevancies yet was able to suggest a complete world. In a very different way, he found himself drawn to Faulkner's willfully convoluted, defiantly unpolished style. By means of this covert subtlety of manner, Faulkner's novels of the Deep South seemed able to include every aspect of simple rural life while somehow conferring on it the timeless grandeur of heroic myth. García Márquez began writing a novel of his own, which drew on the stories of Aracataca that he had heard in his childhood. Mindful of his grandmother's description of such times, he called his novel *Leaf Storm*.

Around the end of 1949, García Márquez moved from Cartagena north to Barranquilla, the most lively and cosmopolitan of the coastal cities. This was where the steamers that traded more than three hundred miles into the interior along the Magdalena River berthed alongside the coasters that plied between the Caribbean islands, as well as larger freighters from the Atlantic and, through the Panama Canal, from the Pacific. The population included communities of Jewish refugees from Europe, German and French businessmen, and Spanish traders as well as the indigenous Caribbean mix of African, South American Indian, and Spanish colonials. García Márquez was taken on by the local newspaper *El Heraldo*. He wrote a daily article under the heading "El Jirafa" (The Giraffe), so called because the column in which it was printed was long and thin like a giraffe's neck. More important for the future, he was also put in charge of the foreign desk. Here he began to gain a wider understanding of the Latin American situation and its role in the larger scheme of things. By now a more gregarious character, he soon drifted into a circle of young intellectuals. These would-be writers and artists would argue and discuss literature into the early hours in their favorite haunt, the Japi Bar (phonetic Spanish for "Happy Bar"). With characteristic exaggeration, García Márquez would later remember: "We would drink until daylight, talking literature. Every night at least ten books I hadn't read came up in conversation, and on the next day they would lend them to me."

But García Márquez also found himself mixing once again with a wide range of colorful street characters—seamen, pimps, taxi drivers, lorry drivers—listening wide-eyed to their fantastic tales. He found accommodation in the four-story block known as El Rascacielos (literally The Skyscraper), on a street that had once been known colloquially, and was now known officially, as Calle del Crimen (Crime Street). The first two floors of El Rascacielos contained a lawyer's office; the floors above this were a brothel, where García Márquez would be given a cheap bed in any room that remained unused when he returned from his nights at the Japi Bar. He was constantly broke during this period. His pay as a journalist was not high, and he was frequently behind on his rent, even at the cut-rate he was allowed at El Rascacielos. Until he came up with the money, he would be forced to leave behind as security his "most precious possession"— the manuscript of his novel *Leaf Storm*, which he continued to work on.

During this period García Márquez had a brief fling with an Afro-Hispanic prostitute called Eufemia who worked at El Rascacielos. The incident would be put to comic effect in a later work, where a large prostitute called Nigromanta seduces an absentminded bibliophile who is a virgin. In fact, García Márquez already had a girlfriend in Barranquilla. This was "the beautiful Mercedes," whom he had first met when he was a seventeen-year-old schoolboy home on holiday. He had been invited to a dance, where he had immediately been attracted to the thirteen-year-old Mercedes, who was the daughter of a neighbor. He developed a crush on her, but she had not been so impressed with her gauche suitor. By now her family had moved to Barranquilla, which remained comparatively peaceful through *La Violencia*, and she proved a little more sympathetic when she encountered the raffish young journalist who wrote "El Jirafa." She became his "secret girlfriend," and when they were together he referred to her as "crocodilo sagrado" (sacred crocodile)—either because her ancestry was partly Egyptian or because he thought her expression sometimes resembled that of a crocodile (García Márquez is wont to claim either).

Now García Márquez finally completed his novel *Leaf Storm*. This he packed up and sent off with high hopes to the Buenos Aires publisher Losada, which had been recommended to him by one of his intellectual friends. After a long wait, it was returned. Inside he found a brutal rejection letter, telling him: "You have not sufficient talent to become a genuine writer. I recommend you concentrate on taking up another career." Ironically, the letter had been written by the brother-in-law of García Márquez's hero, Borges.

This letter had a devastating effect on Márquez. At the end of 1952 he gave up his job at *El Heraldo* and simply disappeared from Barranquilla. What he did during the ensuing year remained for a long time a mystery which he preferred to gloss over. It is now known that the twenty-five-year-old traveled the Caribbean coastal region as an unsuccessful encyclopedia salesman, a deeply humiliating experience which drove him to the edge of despair.

At about this time, García Márquez accompanied his mother on a journey back to Aracataca in order to sell the house where he had lived with his grandfather. This proved a traumatic experience. He had not been back to Aracataca for ten years, and as he walked down the empty main street in the overwhelming heat of the afternoon he felt he was returning to a "ghost town. . . . I had the sensation that the entire town was dead, including the living." When they arrived at the house, he found that the home he remembered from childhood had been transformed. During the last years of his grandmother's life, she had become demented; and in her blind state, conversing with the living and the dead, she had neglected the house and its garden. Lost in her solitude, she had been unaware that the almond trees were being devoured by ants, the flowers were rotting, the garden turning into a wasteland.

Later on this same visit, García Márquez listened to the local pharmacist tell his mother the stories of all that had happened since he had left. He found himself overwhelmed with a feeling of the circularity of everything that had taken place in the town, as if its stories were welling up out of a nothingness to which they would eventually return. Yet he was also aware that these stories contained a reality that was missing in the stories he told in his own writing. Compared to them, his writing was a literary confectionery, nothing but an intellectual construction. What these stories had—despite all their exaggerations, non sequiturs and implausibilities—was a reality of their own, which was a poetical transformation of the reality they sought to describe. This was what he should have been aiming at in his writing, not just the lessons learned from his great predecessors.

Now, as he traveled from town to town selling his encyclopedias, he began listening to the stories he was told—in the bars and shops and homes—with fresh ears. He would later claim that many of these stories, from all over the Caribbean region, appeared in *One Hundred Years of Solitude* almost exactly as he remembered hearing them. The history of Macondo was beginning to take shape in his head.

In 1954 García Márquez returned to Bogotá, where he obtained a post on *El Espectador*. The Liberal newspaper was undergoing a difficult period. The dictator Gustavo Rojas Pinilla had seized power in a military coup the preceding year, and he resented the constant sniping in the press about him and his regime. García Márquez was appointed a staff reporter, which guaranteed him a regular wage. His main job was as the paper's regular film critic, the first such post in a Colombian newspaper. He took his job very seriously, as did his employers and his readers, despite his confident prediction in his column that the days of the cinema as a medium would soon be over. He was also sent on an occasional assignment, writing larger pieces on such topics as the collapse of a hotel in Medellín or the life of a famous Colombian cyclist. This aspect of his work led him to become, unexpectedly, the most famous journalist in Colombia.

Early in March 1955, a twenty-year-old Colombian sailor called Luis Alejandro Velasco was discovered washed up on a remote northern beach, more dead than alive. Ten days earlier he had been blown overboard from a Colombian navy destroyer during a fierce tropical storm, along with seven other sailors, all of whom had been reported missing. Velasco had spent ten days adrift on a raft in the Caribbean without food or water. Overnight he became a national hero and was even given a medal by the president, who made sure that he capitalized on this event. Despite this attention, Velasco found that his moment of fame was soon over, whereupon he was unceremoniously discarded by the authorities. Consequently he turned up at the offices of *El Espectador*, offering to tell the full story of his ordeal at sea, and was passed on to García Márquez. Over the next few days, García Márquez listened as Velasco, "a born storyteller," recounted his tale. The Colombian destroyer on which he was serving had set out from Mobile, Alabama, after a refit which had taken eight months to complete. Just two hours from journey's end at Cartagena, the destroyer had encountered a heavy swell and strong winds—not the fierce tropical storm previously reported. At one point the ship had lurched, some cargo on deck had broken loose, and eight sailors had been swept overboard. The destroyer had begun listing because of the displaced deck cargo, and had thus been unable to turn in time to rescue the men lost overboard. García Márquez asked Velasco about the cargo. Not only was it forbidden to carry cargo on the deck of a destroyer, because it unbalanced the ship; this had been contraband—American radios, washing machines, and refrigerators to be sold in Colombia. As García Márquez later wrote: "It was clear that the tale, like the destroyer, also carried an ill-secured political and moral cargo which had not been foreseen."

García Márquez's serialization appeared in Velasco's name, under the heading: "The Truth

About My Adventure." In fourteen episodes, skillfully paced by García Márquez, each episode left the reader wanting to know what happened next. The public was soon gripped by Velasco's tale, living every moment as he survived on his life raft under the blazing Caribbean sun. They too became indignant that the life raft had been improperly maintained and had no emergency rations. During the first days, passing search planes had failed to spot Velasco on his raft— then there were no more planes. A few ships passed, but they too did not notice him. Each day at the same time the sharks would begin to circle the raft, and one even bit through an oar. Velasco had no water but managed to snare a seagull, which he found he could not bring himself to eat. Instead he chewed on some American store brochures that he had kept in his pocket as a souvenir.

In no time the entire country was following Velasco's story, episode by episode, right through to its enthralling end. The president and the authorities were less enthralled, and put great pressure on Velasco to retract his story. But he refused. As a result he was later sacked from the navy, and the onetime national hero vanished into obscure poverty. (Over ten years later, García Márquez tracked him down and belatedly made amends for this. By now world-famous, he wrote a book on Velasco's story but insisted that all the royalties go to "the anonymous compatriot who had to endure ten days on a raft without eating or drinking, in order to make this book possible.")

Other events following the serialization of Velasco's story in *El Espectador* were similarly double-edged. The paper's circulation rose spectacularly, but the dictator Rojas Pinilla now had a score to settle. When news leaked that García Márquez had ghost-written the story, he quickly became the most famous journalist in Colombia. But the editor of *El Espectador* realized that this placed García Márquez in some danger, and sent him abroad for his own safety. In July 1955 García Márquez was dispatched to Geneva as *El Espectador*'s new correspondent for Europe.

He was now twenty-seven, and as he left he just had time to write to Mercedes asking her to wait for him. Unaware of what lay in store, he promised her he would be back in a few months when things had blown over, and then they would get married. She agreed. At the same time another portentous event took place. By now García Márquez had already had a number of short stories published in various papers, but at last a small publisher in Bogotá had agreed to publish his greatly rewritten novel *Leaf Storm*. The book was duly published, but around the same time the publisher disappeared, leaving García Márquez to pay the printer's bills. He just had time to peddle a few copies on the street before he was sent abroad. Not until four years later, at the Colombia Book Fair, would *Leaf Storm* begin to attract real attention.

Leaf Storm opens: "—Suddenly, as if a whirlwind had set down roots in the center of the town, the banana company arrived, pursued by the leaf storm . . . formed out of the human and material dregs of other towns, the chaff of civil war. . . ." From the very beginning, García Márquez would always set great store by the opening sentence of each work he wrote. Later he would claim that sometimes these had taken him longer to write than the entire work: "Because the sentence can be the laboratory for testing the style, the structure and even the length of the book." But having finally arrived at his opening sentence, he does not simply leap in headlong. He always makes sure that he has a picture of what the book is to be about. "I always start with an image. In *Leaf Storm*, it's an old man taking his grandson to a funeral."

As with many first novels, aspects of *Leaf Storm* are derivative, owing a huge debt to its author's literary heroes—in this case, William Faulkner, and in particular the two works he wrote at the end of the 1920s, *The Sound and the Fury* and *As I Lay Dying*. The first of these consists entirely of a number of monologues, by various characters, and is set in Faulkner's fictional Deep South home, Yoknapatawpha County, in rural Mississippi. *As I Lay Dying* uses the same technique, with the various voices accompanying a coffin on its way to be buried. Most of *Leaf Storm* consists of three voices as they wait by a coffin in a house in García

Márquez's own fictional hometown of Macondo. But what makes the book special is how it manages to rise above its obvious sources.

The three voices that form the bulk of the book are those of the Colonel, his daughter Isabel, and her son, who is approaching his eleventh birthday. García Márquez himself has admitted that the Colonel is based, as clearly as he knew how, upon his own grandfather. The weak and abandoned thirty-year-old mother is not his mother, but there is no doubting that her young son has much of the author in him. Too much, one might say. Some of the perceptions of this nameless child are certainly not those of a ten-year-old: "the walls will crumble, but noiselessly, like a palace of ash collapsing in the wind." The sheer imagination of such lines perhaps makes them forgivable.

The overall setting of the novel is the hot midafternoon gloom of a house closely resembling the one in which García Márquez grew up. It is 1928, the year of the author's birth and the year when the striking banana plantation workers were shot down by the army. An open coffin sits in the room, and in it lies the dead body of an unnamed French doctor, a drifter who had arrived in Macondo in 1903. He had set up a thriving practice, but this had fallen into decline with the arrival of the banana company doctors. After this, the doctor gradually declined into a bitter recluse—though he retained a curious relationship with the Colonel. On the morning preceding the novel's action, he has hanged himself. The small-minded townsfolk are against burying a suicide, but the Colonel feels obscurely obliged to have the doctor properly buried. The three internal monologues around the coffin ponder what is happening, reminiscing to themselves about the events that have occurred over the years leading up to this scene.

The book begins at two-thirty in the afternoon, when the boy hears the distant whistle of the two-thirty train. It ends half an hour later, when the boy hears a single curlew begin to sing somewhere in the town. He has been told that curlews sing when they smell a dead man. The coffin is nailed closed and then carried out of the house. The last words of the book are the boy's:

"Now they'll get the smell. Now all the curlews will start to sing." Implied, but not described, is the ensuing defiance of the townsfolk by the Colonel, whose wishes concerning the coffin are about to be fulfilled.

Despite its flaws and blatant influences, *Leaf Storm* would later be recognized by a few perceptive critics as the first sounding of an entirely original voice, one that would mark the birth of a new modernism in Latin American literature. But all this still lay some years in the future when García Márquez flew from Colombia into European exile in 1955.

He was now comparatively well off, with a regular monthly paycheck of two hundred dollars. Although he had none of the support to which European and North American foreign correspondents were accustomed, he was free to roam the continent. For the most part he was forced to work alone, cobbling together regular reports from other journalistic sources. But he did cover the 1956 four-power summit conference in Geneva firsthand, and wrote a series of articles on the aging Pope Pius XII, who is best remembered for the silence he maintained with regard to Nazi treatment of the Jews during World War II. García Márquez's readership back in Colombia was Roman Catholic, and he chose to take an evenhanded approach to the pope. Yet concentrating on Pius XII must have had some effect, for it was around this time that he first became intrigued by the personalities of figures who wielded great power—especially that epitome of power and its corruptive influence, the Latin American dictator. (At this time around a dozen Latin American countries were ruled by more or less vicious dictators—countries ranging from Argentina to Venezuela, including ogres such as Batista of Cuba and Stroessner of Paraguay.) Perhaps inevitably, García Márquez's view of European politics was colored by the struggles of the left in his home continent. As a result, his journalism sometimes suffered from lapses of judgment. After the 1956 uprising against the Communist regime in Hungary, for example, his attempt at "evenhandedness" was sadly farcical.

García Márquez eventually based himself in Paris, where he found many Latin American political exiles. Here he received the news that *El Espectador* had been closed down by the regime. He decided against going back, cashed in his return ticket, and rented a seventh-floor garret on the Rue Cajas in the heart of the Latin Quarter, intent on writing a book. These were lean times, and he was soon struggling to bring in any cash at all as a freelance journalist. He often went hungry and soon lost weight. When his mother received a photograph of him, she cried out that he looked "like a ghost." Worse still, his swarthy Latin American complexion made him look like an Algerian, at least to the police. The Algerian war of independence had begun, and Algerians were planting bombs in Paris. When García Márquez was challenged by the police in Arabic, he was unable to answer—"*les flics*" saw this as resistance and reacted accordingly. He was several times roughed up by the police and spent more than one night in a police cell.

García Márquez holed up in his garret room, wrapped in rags against the cold, and began writing through the long nights, going through two packs of cheap, pungent French cigarettes a session. His writing eventually became a novella entitled *No One Writes to the Colonel*, based on the experience of his grandfather, who had waited in vain for his military pension. But it is not difficult to see how García Márquez also read his own perilous situation into the story. Sometimes he was now reduced to begging on the streets, at other times he sang Mexican songs in cafés for handouts. Whenever he could, he continued writing.

No One Writes to the Colonel is composed in a very different style from *Leaf Storm*. García Márquez had asked himself, "How can I keep on working in this mythical field and with this poetical style, in the circumstances that we're living through? It seems like an evasion." The circumstances he was referring to were of course *La Violencia*, which provides a menacing background to his new work. Remaining true to his intention, García Márquez severely curbs the poetical style that had been so hard-won and now appeared to come almost naturally to him. Instead he adopted a precise, unfussy, sober style. The effect is cinematic in its precision, journalistic in its clarity. The spare style is well matched to his subject matter.

The book begins with the Colonel prying open the coffee tin in his kitchen and seeing that only a small spoonful of grounds remains. "He scraped the inside of the tin with a knife until the last scrapings of the ground coffee, mixed with bits of rust, poured into the pot." In coffee-rich Colombia, such circumstances bespeak deep poverty. The seventy-five-year-old Colonel and his aging wife have nothing. And their physical state is little better than their material state. They both suffer from the ailments of old age: she is visited by the doctor for her asthma while he endures his constipation. And with humorous obstinacy he continues hoping that one day his pension will arrive. Each Friday he dutifully goes down to the port, waiting for the postboat that has made the eight-hour journey along the river, or he goes to the post office. Each time it is the same. No one writes to the Colonel.

Two months before the opening of the novel, the Colonel's son Augustin has been murdered at the cockfight pit. The son has been the sole support of his aged mother and father, and as the Colonel's wife tellingly remarks: "We are the orphans of our son." But the son has left them something—his fighting cock. The Colonel's wife insists that the cockerel should be sold to provide something for them to eat, but the Colonel refuses. The cockerel is their future. If they train it properly, it will be ready to fight in a few weeks' time and will make them a fortune when it wins. His wife continues nagging, but he insists:

> "He's worth his weight in gold," he said. . . .
> "You can't eat illusions," the woman said.
> "You can't eat them, but they sustain you," the colonel replied.

This is the crux of the story. The Colonel refuses to be ground down by his adverse circumstances. His plight is further deepened into the plight of the country by successive, insistent hints of *La Violencia*. There is a nightly curfew at eleven o'clock, references to films censored by the church, the lack of elections, the censorship of the newspapers. When the doctor visits the house to treat the Colonel's wife, he gives the Colonel a mimeographed sheet of paper, telling him to circulate it. This is the clandestine news sheet of the revolutionaries, conveying the "real" news of resistance to the regime.

But in the midst of it all the Colonel gently persists in his "illusion." He is old, gentle in his manner, and fleetingly aware of the absurdity and humor of his situation. His wife persists in her own different way. When they haven't eaten for days, she tells him: "Several times I've put stones on to boil, so the neighbors wouldn't know we've gone for days without putting the pot on the stove." In moments of respite, their son's friends give the Colonel's wife corn mash for the cockerel, to keep it in fighting shape. The Colonel comes home and remarks on the meal of corn mash she has set before him.

"Where'd it come from?"
"From the rooster," the woman answered. "The boys brought him so much corn that he decided to share it with us. That's life."

As the novel approaches its end, the situation remains unresolved. The Colonel and his wife are still living in penury, the cockfight remains some way in the future, and there is still no sign of the Colonel's pension. But a subtle change has taken place. Threatening clouds and incessant rain have given way to clear skies. A circus has arrived in town, prompting the Colonel to memories of better times. He decides to ignore his wife's nagging and even takes a side street so as to avoid going to the post office. In the final scene his wife loses patience with him, demanding:

"And meanwhile what do we eat?"

As she seizes him and shakes him by the collar, the Colonel comes to a realization: "It had taken the colonel seventy-five years—seventy-five years of his life, minute by minute—to reach this moment. He felt pure, explicit, invincible at the moment when he replied:

"'Shit.'"

It is as if the Colonel's final exclamation resonates back through all that has taken place—referring ironically to his constipation, commenting on the microcosm of their lives as well as the macrocosm of *La Violencia*. Yet coming from the gentle, gently spoken colonel, with his aversion to profanity, it is a realization of his inner defiance.

In 1957 García Márquez received a telegram offering him a post on a magazine in Caracas, Venezuela. A friend had remembered him. Within days of his arrival there, the Venezuelan military rose against the dictator General Marcos Pérez Jiménez. With his friend, he watched from the window as fighter planes flew over the rooftops, strafing the presidential palace. That night, as they listened to the radio in an attempt to find out what was happening, they saw a single military transport plane flying over the darkened city out toward the coast. This was Jiménez, leaving for exile, accompanied by suitcases stuffed with millions of dollars. (In the rush to board the plane, one of his henchmen left on the tarmac a briefcase containing $11 million.) Days later, García Márquez was with other journalists in the presidential palace as the new junta deliberated behind closed doors. He struck up a conversation with the major domo of the presidential palace who had served at his post for fifty years, watching presidents and dictators come and go. He had even served throughout the reign of the notorious tyrant General Juan Vicente Gómez. García Márquez listened in fascination to the recounting of private details, anecdotes, and personal foibles of the man who for twenty-seven years (1908–1935) had exercised absolute power over Venezuela.

A few months later García Márquez flew back to Colombia. By now the military dictatorship had been overthrown, and the elites of the Conservative and Liberal parties had reached an agreement which resulted in the so-called National Front. This amalgam was a curious democratic fantasy, astonishing even by Latin American standards. The two parties jointly decided that elections should be held on a regular basis. In order to avoid the usual violence associated with this democratic process, the results would be decided in advance. All seats in both houses of Congress would be evenly divided between the two parties, with no other parties being permitted. Likewise, the ministers and provincial governorships would also be evenly divided, and the presidency would alternate between the two parties every four years. This equality between the two parties was to be strictly maintained from top to bottom, including local municipal assemblies and even the number of political prisoners each side could incarcerate of the opposing party. This highly original, but in practice highly repressive, political arrangement would be dubbed "the world's first attempt at a two-party dictatorship."

García Márquez now embarked upon what many see as a similar arrangement in the personal sphere—he married. His "secret girlfriend" Mercedes had proved as good as her word, faithfully waiting for him through thick and thin. García Márquez was now thirty years old, and he optimistically promised his new bride: "By the time I am forty, I am going to write my greatest masterpiece."

Early in 1959 an event occurred that would change the face of Latin American politics—it would also transform the life of García Márquez. This was the Cuban Revolution, when

Fidel Castro and his band of guerrillas (including Che Guevara) swept down from the mountains, overthrew the dictator Fulgencio Batista, and ultimately established the first Communist state in the Western Hemisphere. The United States mounted a propaganda campaign against Cuba, and in retaliation Castro set up the first Latin American press agency: Prensa Latina. García Márquez was soon invited to join, and began working from Havana. These were exhilarating days for a young left-wing idealist. The Cuban Revolution was in its infancy and became a symbol of hope for people who were suffering under corrupt and repressive regimes throughout Latin America. Castro began implementing long-overdue reforms; he also nationalized many extensive American banana and sugar plantations. Heady with power, the Cuban leader began delivering long rhetorical speeches attacking America, and established close links with the Soviet Union. García Márquez was highly sympathetic. In his own words: "I want the world to be socialist, and I believe that sooner or later it will be." But there is no doubt he had reservations, the extent of which is difficult to tell. At times, his silence would make his reservations appear minimal.

When *No One Writes to the Colonel* was published in 1959, it received some sympathetic reviews but otherwise caused no great stir. García Márquez also had a son; he now had a family to support—and protect. During his spell as New York correspondent for *La Prensa*, he received death threats, and Mercedes decided she was unwilling to bring up a family under such circumstances. In 1961, they settled in Mexico City, where García Márquez worked as a scriptwriter for Mexican films and edited a women's magazine. This brought him money, but it was hardly a successful period for him artistically. He felt he was at a dead end. Having finally saved up five thousand dollars, he sat down to write the masterpiece he had sworn to produce before he was forty.

In his own words, the aim of this book would be "to find a way of expressing in literature all the experiences which had influenced me in some way as a child." The experience of writing it would prove cathartic. This was the work that would eventually become *One Hundred Years of Solitude*.

As with so many of his works, the opening sentence is germinal as well as inspirational: "Many years later, as he faced the firing squad, Colonel Aureliano Buendia was to remember that distant afternoon when his father took him to discover ice." *One Hundred Years of Solitude* is a history of Macondo, from its origins in earliest colonial times to the middle of the twentieth century. This is no factual, linear history, though its magical narrative recognizably coexists with "real" history. Its central theme is the saga of the Buendia family, whose patriarch Jose Arcadio Buendia and his cousin-wife Ursula Iguaran first ventured across the sierra to found Macondo. In its earliest incarnation, Macondo was "a village of twenty adobe houses built on the banks of a river of crystal water rushing over a bed of stones—polished, white and enormous like prehistoric eggs. The world was so recent that many things lacked a name. . . ."

Every year in March the village was visited by a family of ragged gypsies who pitched tents on the outskirts "with a great uproar of pipes and kettledrums." They brought with them the latest inventions from the outside world—a magnet, later false teeth, also "a magnifying glass the size of a drum" which was "the latest discovery of the Jews of Amsterdam." The gypsies were led by the wise Melquiades, "with an untamed beard and sparrow hands." He was a magus, expert in all kinds of knowledge, from alchemy to ancient languages. Some of this knowledge he passed on to Jose Arcadio Buendia, who became so interested in science that "he spent the long months of the rainy season shut up in a small room . . . so that no one would disturb his experiments."

At one stage Jose Arcadio Buendia mounted an expedition, heading north into the jungle, in an attempt to form a link with civilization. But as they pressed on, the vegetation became "thicker and thicker" while around them rose "the cries of the birds and the uproar of the monkeys." They progressed "like sleepwalkers through a universe of grief, lighted only by the tenuous reflection of luminous insects, and their lungs were overwhelmed by a suffocating smell of blood." After two weeks, one morning they awoke to find: "Before them, surrounded by ferns and palm trees, white and powdery in the silent morning light, was an enormous Spanish galleon." Its masts and ragged sails were "adorned with orchids. The hull covered with an armor of petrified barnacles and soft moss." When the members of the expedition ventured cautiously inside its hulk, they found "nothing but a thick forest of flowers."

Jose Arcadio Buendia has two sons, Aureliano and Jose Arcadio, who represent the two differing characteristics that will recur in the Buendia family tree. Each of them in turn has a child by the lustful Pilar Ternera. Jose Arcadio later disappears with the gypsies. The other son becomes the fearsome and absurd Colonel Aureliano Buendia, whose memory of ice opens the novel. Colonel Aureliano is a local despot who has started no less than thirty-three revolutionary wars against the government, and succeeded in losing every one of them. Among other things, he has survived numerous ambushes, fourteen attempted assassinations, and even the firing squad. He has also succeeded in fathering seventeen illegitimate sons with seventeen different women. Later these seventeen sons all turn up in Macondo with their mothers. It is one of these bastards who brings a train to Macondo, and this brings the foreign banana company. In its wake comes corruption and the violence that eventually kills all seventeen of the Colonel's illegitimate sons. And so the magical tale continues. . . .

Amidst this wide swath of history, the town has its own "historic" events. The shaman Melquiades becomes the first person to die in Macondo, "for Macondo was a town that was unknown to the dead until Melquiades arrived and marked it with a small black dot on the many-colored maps of death." A priest arrives and establishes the church. The arrival of the magistrate Apolinar Mascote signals the arrival of the law. These events, and several others, bear a strong resemblance to the historical development of Yoknapatawpha County that takes place in Faulkner's novels. Other happenings are recognizable from the Aracataca of García Márquez's childhood, but still others are wholly fantastical. A chocolate-drinking priest levitates. Macondo is rained on by flowers "so that the streets were carpeted with a compact layer that had to be cleared away with shovels and rakes." Its inhabitants suffer from a plague of insomnia and forgetfulness which is first brought to the village by two Indians of royal blood, who end up working as servants in the Buendia's house.

This plague reaches such proportions that Aureliano Buendia becomes afraid he will soon forget the name of even the simplest household items. He begins writing labels and tying them to the objects around him. Soon people throughout the village are labeling their chairs and doors, and even their clocks. Finally Jose Arcadio Buendia hangs a label around the neck of his cow, saying what it is and giving instructions that "she must be milked every day so that she will produce milk." And such is everyone's forgetfulness that even this requires further instructions: "the milk must be boiled so that it can be mixed with coffee to make coffee with milk." Although knowledge of everyday reality fades before the towns-folk's forgetfulness, it can be retained by words.

This plague is only halted with the arrival of Melquiades in Macondo. Although he has died, he has come back to the land of the living "because he cannot bear the solitude" of the dead. Melquiades has a magic potion that frees the minds of the villagers from their forgetfulness and for the time being cures them of their plague. But Melquiades pays heavily for his preference for the living reality of Macondo over the solitude of death. He quickly grows old and hides himself away in a room filled with books and manuscripts in the Buendia house. Here he begins writing a series of coded manuscripts, in a script no one has ever seen before. Apparently he is writing down "everything that was recordable in Macondo."

At one point the lascivious Pilar Ternera understands "the history of the Buendia family is a chain of irreparable repetitions, a gyrating wheel that would have continued turning forever had it not been for the gradual and inevitable wearing out of the axle." It is she who is responsible for the continuation of the Buendias' line, by having a child by both Aureliano and Jose Arcadio. At times she appears almost like a priestess, yet she also runs a brothel. The novel contains a plethora of erotic incidents and leitmotifs. People are continually falling in love or in lust. Most of the men visit brothels at one time or another; a few prefer the chaste methods of traditional Spanish courtship. We witness teenage crushes, violence, and even conjugal love. At one point one of the many Aurelianos who recur regularly in the Buendia family tree dashes about the house "balancing a beer bottle on his inconceivable organ." At the other end of the scale, Colonel Aureliano Buendia's sister Amaranta remains an angst-ridden virgin, who spends her time rebuffing those who desire her and longs only for men who are unattainable to her.

The history of Macondo is one of irreversible decline and degeneration. Much of this is reflected in the decline of the Buendia family, but Macondo itself is hit most damagingly by the banana company, which introduces its own corruption. Reflecting actual historical events, this situation comes to a head with a strike which is brutally repressed with a massacre of the workers. After this the banana company leaves, an event followed by continuous rain and floods which last for four years, eleven months, and two days. They seem to be caused by the banana company to avoid negotiations with the workers.

Among the last generations of the Buendia family we encounter the young and playful Renata Remedios (Meme), who has an affair with Mauricio Babilonia, a local garage mechanic. The result is yet another Aureliano. He grows up to become a young man who spends half his life reading and the other half carousing with his intellectual friends in the brothels and arguing about literature. In the mornings, at home in the Buendia's house, he hides himself away in a book-filled room. Here he teaches himself everything out of an encyclopedia, and in addition learns "Sanskrit . . . English and French, and a little Latin and Greek." In the room he comes across some ancient, faded manuscripts. As he tries to decipher them, he realizes that they are the manuscripts left by Melquiades. Around this time he falls in love with his aunt Amaranta Ursula. She betrays her husband to have passionate incest with her nephew. "They would roll around naked in the mud of the courtyard, and one afternoon they almost drowned as they made love in the water tank. . . . They destroyed the furniture in the parlor, in their madness they tore to shreds the hammock . . . and they disemboweled the mattresses and emptied them on the floor as they suffocated in storms of cotton." Amaranta Ursula becomes pregnant and eventually gives birth to a son, who is born with a pig's tail. But soon after giving birth she dies of a hemorrhage.

Despite all the sexual shenanigans that take place in Macondo, Aureliano and Amaranta Ursula are the only two who have shared a genuine love for each other. Consequently Aureliano is utterly devastated by the death of Amaranta Ursula. Afterward he "wandered aimlessly through the town, searching for an entrance that went back to the past." He ends up "in the last open saloon of the tumbledown red light district, where an accordion is playing. . . . The bartender, who had a withered and somewhat bent arm because he had raised it to strike his mother, invited Aureliano to have a bottle of cane liquor." Aureliano ends up drunk and weeping, and finally returns home to find that his baby son has been abandoned, and has become a "bloated bag of skin that all the ants in the world were dragging toward their holes along the stone path in the garden." His son is dead, but "at that prodigious instant" he has a flash of understanding.

"Aureliano had never been more lucid in any act of his life": he realizes what Melquiades's manuscripts are about. Emptying his mind of the memory "of his dead ones and the pain of his dead ones," he returns home. He nails up the door, boarding himself up in the room with the manuscripts, which he finds "intact among the prehistoric plants and steaming puddles and luminous insects that had removed all trace of man's passage on earth from the room." The manuscripts contain a poem describing "the history of his family, written by Melquiades, down to the most trivial happenings, one hundred years before they had taken place. He had written it in

Sanskrit, which was his mother tongue, and he had encoded the even lines in the cipher of the Emperor Augustus and the odd ones in the military code of Sparta."

Aureliano begins reading and finds "that Melquíades had not set down events in the order that human beings lived time, but had concentrated a century of daily episodes in such a way that they existed simultaneously in a single instant." And so the manuscript begins telling the history of the Buendia family. But Aureliano grows impatient, skipping ahead because he wants to find out about his own origins. He becomes so absorbed in his reading that he does not notice that outside the house a wind is blowing up "full of voices from the past, the murmurs of ancient geraniums." Then he finds what he is looking for: "the instant of his own conception among the scorpions and the yellow butterflies in a sunset bathroom where a mechanic satisfied his lust on a woman who was giving herself away out of rebellion." Still absorbed, Aureliano does not notice that by now there had been a second, greater gust of wind "whose cyclonic strength tore the doors and windows off their hinges, pulled off the roof of the east wing, and uprooted the foundations." He skips the next pages containing his own past life, which he knows all too well, until he comes to the final pages where he "began to decipher the instant that he was living, deciphering it as he lived it, prophesying himself in the act of deciphering the last pages of the manuscript." Before reaching it, he already knows the final line: "he had already understood that he would never leave that room." He knows that he, and all that he has read about, will disappear forever "because races condemned to one hundred years of solitude did not have a second chance on earth."

The closing scenes of *One Hundred Years of Solitude* have an extraordinary power, both poetic and narrative, as they move toward a climax that gradually becomes inevitable. This ending continues to resonate long after one has finished reading it. There are, of course, the trivial structuralist considerations—such as whether the entire narrative is merely Melquiades's writing, or whether the objective narrative voice originates elsewhere. These are best left to literary sleuths. The main effect is that the ending causes one to ponder and recollect the entire narrative. This is a poignant moment which makes one reflect on the "solitude" that has enveloped all the inhabitants of Macondo throughout its history.

Yet for some critics this ending has its flaws—the very same flaws that mar the entire work. The inevitability of this finale is somewhat undermined by its very poetry. Inevitability and fantasy do not mix well. With García Márquez's brand of fantasy, there is always the feeling that anything could happen. The often fantastic reality of Borges, whose influence lies heavy over these last scenes, is conveyed in a lapidary prose; it is recounted in a sober tone of classical restraint. García Márquez's more poetic lyrical tone is beguiling but to some minds not always altogether convincing. Yet there is no denying its evocative power. And ultimately one is either enthralled from the word go, and thus easily led, or one remains unconvinced by his poetic reality. The suspension of disbelief, so necessary for all art, becomes more difficult when this art attempts to convince us of something other than a recognizable reality. How can people be condemned to anything, let alone García Márquez's version of solitude, when they inhabit a reality that is capable of breaking free of any reality? Once again, such questions can be asked only in the sober light of day, from outside our actual experiencing of the narrative. If one is convinced by the "magical" narration, one accepts García Márquez on his own terms.

For those who fall under García Márquez's spell, the journey undertaken in *One Hundred Years of Solitude* is one of the richest literary dreams ever written. More than one European critic has likened García Márquez's masterpiece to an extended prose equivalent of Coleridge's *Kubla Khan*. But this history of Macondo is no opium dream: García Márquez's dream is inhabited by real—if occasionally dreamlike—people involved in quasi-realistic events. And what is more, it is possible to recognize their counterparts in reality.

This was the recognition that so enthused his earliest readers. Here was an echo of their own personal, political, domestic, and even existential Latin American reality. Never before had such justice been done to the world in which they lived, with everything from its trivialities to its tragedies. There had long been an element of "magic realism" in Latin American literature, but García Márquez had made this his own. Soon his version of "magic realism" was sweeping the world, influencing readers and writers alike from Paris to Moscow, from New York to Tokyo. As *One Hundred Years of Solitude* was translated into foreign languages, it inevitably lost an element that so many of its native readers had recognized. Foreign readers could not see what they did not know. For many such readers, *One Hundred Years of Solitude* portrayed an exotic reality which obscured the suffering that went on in the real world. In the exaggerated world of Macondo, suffering took on an element of unreality. This view García Márquez was anxious to dispel, insisting again and again that "every single line in all my books has a starting point in reality." Yet there is no denying that in *One Hundred Years of Solitude* this rich coloring, often playful manner, and endlessly imaginative vitality, too vibrant to be confined to any scientific reality, can sometimes obscure what García Márquez is at such pains to convey. But once we look beyond this "color" to the life actually reflected here, we cannot fail to see that it is harsh, unforgiving, and offers little comfort to those forced to live it.

Following his worldwide success, García Márquez began to live the life of a famous author. But his political position transcended the banality of such a life. As a man of the left, he championed the cause and was in turn championed by its adherents. He became a personal friend of Fidel Castro of Cuba and François Mitterand of France. Despite efforts to turn him into a propaganda "hero of the left," García Márquez did his best to avoid becoming such an empty stereotype. In Colombia he launched the magazine *Alternativa*, with the express aim of providing a different coverage of the news from that being put forward by the right-wing governments of Latin America and the news agencies of the United States. This remained a dangerous period in Latin American politics. Only a few years earlier, the United States and the Soviet Union had been brought to the brink of nuclear war by the Cuban missile crisis. In 1967 Fidel Castro's friend Che Guevara had been gunned down in the Bolivian jungle, where he had gone to foment revolution on the Latin American mainland. Six years later Chile's elected Marxist president, Salvador Allende, was overthrown in a bloody coup covertly encouraged by the United States. Both sides in this struggle had much to account for, but there is no doubting which side García Márquez supported. With regard to his unwavering stance, it is worth remembering once more what Neruda so often repeated about Latin American politics: "You have to take sides. . . . Either you are with the Cadillacs or you support the people with no schooling and no clothes." Public figures were expected to stand up and be counted. Elsewhere García Márquez has maintained that any attempt to implant either democracy or "the Soviet system" would be "unrealistic." "I believe there are as many alternatives as there are countries in our Americas, including the United States," he has said. "I am convinced that we have to find our own solutions." His most consistent and comprehensible stand has been against what he sees as "interference and imperialism."

But García Márquez has also insisted upon retaining his private artistic life. Locking himself away after *One Hundred Years of Solitude*, he continued to write short stories. Then, in 1973, he produced *The Autumn of the Patriarch*. Here, if it was needed, was final proof that García Márquez was not just a "one book" man. As always, the opening sentence sets the scene and the tone of the book: "Over the weekend the vultures got into the presidential palace by pecking through the screens on the balcony windows and the flapping of their wings stirred up the stagnant time inside, and at dawn on Monday the city awoke out of its lethargy of centuries with the warm, soft breeze of a great man dead and rotting grandeur." The dictator of an unnamed Latin American country has died in his palace overlooking the capital city and the Caribbean. The ensuing pages present flashbacks of the patriarch's reign, as García Márquez's long, serpentine sentences burrow into the psychology of his rule. This is a book about power, scrutinizing both the dictator's use of it and the response it evokes in his cowed people. There is a subtle symbiosis between the ruler and the ruled. The patriarch is crazed, cruel, absurd, and paranoid, a mythical figure ruling amidst the solitude of his palace. Yet in a very real sense he is imprisoned in his own myth, obliged to perform the needs and expectations of the people who depend upon him. They view him with awe and loathing; there are even elements of affection in their fear of him. García Márquez captures perfectly the element of curious intimacy that exists between a tyrant and those he tyrannizes.

The patriarch's rule is a blend of whimsy and grandeur, the mundane and the terrible. His peasant mother hangs out the washing on the presidential balcony. When he invites the "Society of Nations" into the country to investigate an injustice, they find that the prisons have all been closed because there aren't any prisoners. In one of the high points of the book, the patriarch suspects there is yet another plot to overthrow him. He decides that it is being led by his lifelong henchman and friend General Rodrigo de Aguilar, the minister of defense. He works out that the general will overthrow him at a given signal during a banquet. On the night in question the honored guests assemble in the banquet hall, the clock strikes midnight, and "the distinguished General Rodrigo de Aguilar made his entrance stretched out on a silver platter decorated with cauliflower and laurel leaves . . . dressed in his uniform . . . with fourteen pounds of medals on his chest and a sprig of parsley in his mouth." But this is not all. There follows an "exquisite ceremony of carving and serving, and when each plate was filled with an equal portion of minister of defense with piñon-seed stuffing and fragrant herbs, [the patriarch] gave the order to begin, eat heartily, gentlemen."

The book is crammed with incidents and insights as well as images that range from the hilarious to the ingenious. We see the "unofficial collector of tax for the right to walk in the shade," and anyone who has ever witnessed approaching storm clouds at first light in the tropics can only marvel at the exactitude and ingenuity of "the fleeting train music of Bruckner thunder dawns that brought on ruinous floods." Yet for all this agility and orginality, *The Autumn of the Patriarch* is heavy going indeed. It consists of a series of unattributed monologues written in sentences that can sometimes last for pages. There are unnumbered chapters, but no paragraphs, for well over two hundred pages. Confronted with yet another page, yet another slab of unbroken type, the reader quails. The narrative crams incident upon incident, image upon image, in a manner that follows its own time and its own logic. This seemingly endless cornucopia of wonders and delights is conveyed in the style of experimental modernism at its most austere.

So why is *The Autumn of the Patriarch* almost unreadable? For the simple reason that the material seems to demand this very approach. The style does fit the material, and the material justly revels in its setting. It would probably have worked no other way. Here García Márquez was daring enough to follow his artistic instinct. Emboldened by the worldwide sales of *One Hundred Years of Solitude*, he felt free to indulge in an artistic tour de force of the most demanding nature. There is an analogy here with his great modernist predecessor James Joyce. If *One Hundred Years of Solitude* was García Márquez's *Ulysses*, *The Autumn of the Patriarch* can be seen as his *Finnegan's Wake*. Some consider García Márquez's second masterpiece, like Joyce's, an aberration of genius. The former it may be (to many an exasperated reader), but it is also the latter. Genius is not easy. If you want to understand the flavor, import, and even meaning of Latin America's most characteristic figure, the dictator, you will have to make an effort.

The Autumn of the Patriarch was quickly translated into all major languages. Many of García Márquez's readers, who had so welcomed *One Hundred Years of Solitude*, were baffled and disappointed. A number of critics were faintly respectful; but a few critics understood what he was doing and perceptively applauded his daring.

This work also received the greatest possible accolade from the most unexpected source. On one occasion the Panamanian dictator General Omar Torrijos informed a dumbfounded García Márquez: "*The Autumn of the Patriarch* is your best book—we are all just as you describe."

García Márquez's depiction of Macondo conveys to the world the full panoply of Latin American life and history. His evocation of that continent's most characteristic figure holds up a mirror to what has done so much to blight that life and stop that history in its tracks. García Márquez had depicted both sides of Latin American solitude: that of the dictator in his palace, and that of the land in which he has flourished.

Afterword

On its own terms, *The Autumn of the Patriarch* was a success. It also turned out to be a success on the highest literary terms, and within seven years of its publication García Márquez became a worthy recipient of the Nobel Prize. His celebrated Nobel address may be regarded as his credo. In an echo of his literary career, it began by depicting his cultural milieu (all those crazy dictators), but then moved to more difficult territory. Rejecting Eurocentric culture, he declared: "I have no desire to give shape to the ideals of Tonio Kröger, whose dream of a union between the chaste North and a passionate South excited Thomas Mann in this place fifty-three years ago." He then made an impassioned plea on behalf of Latin American culture, both artistic and political: "Why are we greeted unreservedly a recognition of our originality in literature when our attempts, in the face of enormous difficulties, to bring about social change are denied us with all sorts of mistrust?" He rejected "the system of social justice imposed by advanced European nations upon their peoples." At the same time he refused to take the easy way out by blaming imperialism and colonialism for Latin America's plight. The violence and endless suffering in its history was the consequence of "secular injustice and infinite bitterness," not some underhanded historical strategy dreamt up "three thousand leagues distant from our home."

He saw himself as part of a noble Latin American heritage, remembering how eleven years earlier the words of the great Chilean poet Pablo Neruda had illuminated the very room in which he now stood. Three years later Neruda had died in his homeland, in the same city, Santiago, where "A Promethean president embattled in a palace in flames died fighting single-handedly against an army." He then remembered another great American writer who had stood in this room on such a day—William Faulkner, who had set his novels in the hinterland of the shore on the other side of the Caribbean. On that occasion, in 1949, the world had not yet recovered from the effects of World War II, and stood facing the imminent prospect of a third world war. Yet Faulkner had declared, despite everything: "I refuse to admit the end of mankind."

Now the cataclysm that Faulkner had refused to countenance had been reduced to a mere "scientific possibility." Under such circumstances, García Márquez believed that he had a right to hope for a future, where we could create "a minor utopia . . . where the lineal generations of one hundred years of solitude will have at last and forever a second chance on earth."

After the success of the Nobel Prize, García Márquez used his fame in the cause of Latin America, becoming almost a roving ambassador in his attempt to raise the continent's profile and explain its situation. He became even more of an

107

established figure of the left. He did what he could to combat internal injustice and external misconceptions about the "other" America. He was also instrumental in the founding of Habeas, the international human rights organization.

Despite this public activity, he found time to continue his literary activities. At intervals he would retreat, working in isolation on draft after draft of novels and short stories. 1981 had seen the publication of *Chronicle of a Death Foretold.* Although strictly speaking this belongs to the period before the Nobel Prize, it did not circulate through the world in translation until well after it, and played no part in his nomination for the prize. *Chronicle of a Death Foretold* confronts yet another perennial Latin American problem— the very Spanish and very male conception of "honor." The short novel is complex, but its basic story is simple enough. A rich young man called Bayardo San Roman turns up in a nameless small town, where he becomes attracted to Angela Vicario. Eventually they are married, but on the night following their wedding feast the bridegroom returns the bride to the house of her family because she is not a virgin. Angela Vicario's middle-class family is thrown into consternation. Her mother attempts to intimidate Angela into revealing who is responsible. In the course of this inquiry, Angela mentions a young man called Santiago Nasar, the son of a wealthy Arab family. He is judged to have been the guilty party, and for honor's sake Angela's twin brothers Pedro and Pablo decide that they must take their revenge upon the man who has brought dishonor upon their family. They confront Santiago and stab him in front of his house. The murder is witnessed by the local people, who remain horrified by its violence long afterward.

The brothers are sent to prison for three years. Meanwhile Angela is still in love with the husband who has abandoned her. She begins sending him letters, writing to him every week for seventeen years. Then one day Bayardo returns to her; he has the two thousand letters she has written to him, but they are unopened.

This simplified retelling of the story does scant justice to the artful way in which García Márquez manages to present it, which is more concerned with the social effects of the murder on the townsfolk and the people closest involved. He does this by once again telling the tale in such a way that the conventional time sequence is dissolved. As usual, the opening sentence is of vital importance in conveying the drift of the book: "On the day they were going to kill him, Santiago Nasar got up at five-thirty in the morning to wait for the boat the bishop was coming on." It ends with a recounting of the murder. The raison d'être of the book is the narrator's attempt to piece together what happened, and the narrator bears certain resemblances to García Márquez himself. At one point he remarks: "Much later, when I was trying to understand something of myself by selling encyclopedias and medical books. . . ." And elsewhere he reveals that Santiago Nasar and he "had grown up together in school and later on in the same gang at vacation time." This helps give the actions a veracity as well as convincing us of the narrator's involvement. Even so, this work is much more than just a factual murder story. It has rightly been characterized as "a fable of that madness which only obscure principle can produce." Yet although its action has the inevitability of tragedy, García Márquez also manages to convey its pointlessness. He certainly knew of such an incident in his own family, as indeed did so many of his countrymen. *La Violencia* had been much more than a purely political situation in Colombia; it had been fueled by countless revenges. And the violence itself continued long after the political emergency.

A further major work was *Love in the Time of Cholera*, which appeared in 1985. This novel is vividly set in Cartagena, "where nothing had happened for four centuries, except for a slow aging amid the shriveled laurels and rotting lagoons." In many ways it is García Márquez's most conventional and realistic story, expanding over four hundred pages as it covers the span from the mid-1880s to the 1930s. In doing so, it ranges from evocations of the cobbled streets of the ancient viceroy's quarter, as well as a pioneer ballooning episode, through to the visit of Charles Lindbergh, the first man to fly solo across the Atlantic in 1927, who later made a triumphant tour of Latin America.

Once again the bare outline of the main story is simply told. The teenage Florentino Ariza falls in love with Fermina Daza, but her disapproving parents arrange for her to be married to the eligible and aristocratic physician Dr. Juvenal Urbino, who has just returned from living in Paris. Fermina gradually settles into the role of an upper-class wife as her husband grows into middle age. Toward the end of her fifty-year marriage, Fermina wrinkles into old age, and we learn that during the last two decades of their union she and her husband have had no sexual contact. By contrast, after a brief period of spiritual abstinence, Florentino quickly develops a gargantuan sexual appetite, having literally hundreds of affairs. Even at seventy-one, by which time he has lost his hair and his teeth, he is still virile. By now he has become a successful businessman, running the company that owns the boats which ply up and down the Magdalena River. When Dr. Urbino finally dies, Florentino turns up and declares his love for Fermina, who is not immediately enamored by her suitor and remains cautious. But in the end, all is for the best, and they set off together on a riverboat where the old man and the old widow will make love together.

In 1989 García Márquez produced one more major novel. This was *The General in His Labyrinth*, which also featured the Magdalena River, but this time as a river of death. The novel is set in 1830 and recounts the dying of the great liberator of Latin America, Simón Bolívar. García Márquez seeks to rescue Bolívar from the pedestal on which history has placed him, portraying him as a very human being. Bolívar ended up as ruler of Gran Colombia, which he had liberated from Spanish rule. But during his last days, his allies turned on him. He survived an assassination attempt and a military revolt, and then the country began to fall apart. In failing health, Bolívar resigned, left Bogotá, and set off down the Magdalena River for the coast. García Márquez opens the book with Bolívar's parting words: "Let's go. No one loves us here." In the circumstances of Bolívar's death, García Márquez sees "the whole secret of the disaster through which this country is living." The book explores Bolívar's life, but offers no solution. It was not the duty of art to provide solutions. Even the public García Márquez found it impossible to rescue modern-day Colombia as it continued on its violent way. During the 1990s the drug cartel of Medellín amassed great wealth from cocaine smuggled across the Caribbean to the United States, riches that placed the drug barons beyond the power of the central government. At the same time left-wing guerrillas took control of large stretches of the hinterland.

Elsewhere in Latin America, life continued as ever. A powerful new ingredient had now been added to the explosive cocktail of civil life in the continent, namely *futbol* (soccer). The glories and defeats of this game became something akin to life itself to the millions of spectators whose existence was otherwise condemned to futility. In 1969 Honduras and El Salvador actually went to war over a soccer match. In 1986 Argentina was a disgruntled nation, sick of rule by a ramshackle and corrupt military junta. But that year Argentina won the World Cup, and the junta knew they were safe. Argentina was transformed into a proud and jubilant nation, and the junta basked in reflected glory. But once again Colombia made its own characteristic contribution. In 1994 a Colombia player scored an own goal, putting Colombia out of the World Cup. When he returned home, he was shot dead.

Meanwhile García Márquez continued to write, though less than his earlier voluminous output, and continued to do what he could on the public stage. Like so many of his fellow Caribbeans, he has a zest for life and insists upon partaking of all its joys—to which he brings the subtle connoisseurship of an artist. When asked in an interview about his favorite color, he described this as "the yellow of the Caribbean seen from Jamaica at three in the afternoon." The exotic vistas of his native shore are matched by its exotic wild life, yet when asked his favorite bird he replied: "canard à l'orange" (duck in orange sauce).

García Márquez's Chief Works in English Translation

NOTE: Owing to the difference between Spanish and English usage with regard to names, Gabriel García Márquez is sometimes listed in catalogs and bookshops under M for Márquez rather then G for García Márquez.

Leaf Storm (first published in Spanish in 1955)* †
No One Writes to the Colonel (1961)* †
Big Mama's Funeral (1961)
In Evil Hour (1962)
One Hundred Years of Solitude (1967)* †

*starred entries indicate major works
†indicates work discussed in the text

The Story of a Shipwrecked Sailor (1970)[†]
*The Incredible and Sad Tale of Innocent Erendira
    and Her Heartless Grandmother* (1972)*
The Autumn of the Patriarch (1975)*[†]
Ninety Days Behind the Iron Curtain (1979)
Chronicle of a Death Foretold (1981)*[†]
*Clandestine in Chile: The Adventures of Miguel
    Littin* (1985)
Love in the Time of Cholera (1985)*[†]
The General in His Labyrinth (1989)*[†]
Strange Pilgrims: Twelve Stories (1992)
News of a Kidnapping (1996)
Living to Tell the Tale: Memoirs (2002)

Chronology of García Márquez's Life and Times

1927 (or 1928)	Gabriel García Márquez born March 6 in Aracataca in northern Colombia.
1929	Wall Street crash and beginning of worldwide depression.
1936	Gabo's grandfather, the Colonel, dies. He goes to live with his parents.
1939	Outbreak of World War II in Europe.
1941	Japan attacks Pearl Harbor; United States enters World War

	II. García Márquez wins scholarship to Liceo Nacional boarding school at Zipaquira; goes to Bogotá for first time.
1945	World War II ends with defeat of Germany and Japan.
1947	García Márquez enters Bogotá University to study law.
1948	Assassination of Gaitan on street in Bogotá sparks *Bogotaza* riots. *La Violencia* spreads throughout Colombia.
1949	Begins work as journalist on *El Universal* in Cartagena.
1949–1952	Moves to Barranquilla, working on *El Heraldo*.
1953	Works as encyclopedia salesman.
1954	Returns to Bogotá, where he works on *El Espectador*.
1955	His first novel, *Leaf Storm*, is published. Sent to Europe as correspondent for *El Espectador*.

1957	Returns to Latin America to work as journalist in Venezuela.
1959	Fidel Castro ousts dictator Batista in Cuba. García Márquez works for *Le Prensa Latina* in Havana, Bogotá, and New York. Publication of *No One Writes to the Colonel*.
1961	García Márquez settles with family in Mexico City, writing for films and magazines.
1962	Cuban missile crisis brings world to the brink of nuclear war.
1963	President Kennedy assassinated.
1967	Publication of *One Hundred Years of Solitude*.
1969	Honduras and El Salvador go to war over a soccer match.
1971	Pablo Neruda wins Nobel Prize.
1973	Allende overthrown in Chile.
1974	García Márquez founds *Alternativa* magazine in Bogotá.

1975	Publication of *Autumn of the Patriarch*.
1977	Panama Canal returned to Panama.
1982	García Márquez wins Nobel Prize. Britain retakes Falkland Islands (Malvinas) after invasion by Argentina.
1985	Publication of *Love in the Time of Cholera*.
1989	Publication of *The General in his Labyrinth*. Berlin Wall comes down.
1990s	Increasing power of Medellín drug Cartel and left-wing guerillas in Columbia.
1992	North American Free Trade Agreement signed by United States, Mexico, and Canada.
1995	Publication of *The Fragrance of Guava: Conversations*.
2002	Publication of *Living to Tell the Tale: Memoirs*.

Recommended Reading

Gene H. Bell-Villada, *García Márquez: The Man and His Work* (University of North Carolina Press, 1990). The best all-round book on García Márquez's writings—it covers his life, the Colombian context, and all the major novels and short stories.

Regina Janes, *One Hundred Years of Solitude: Modes of Reading* (Twayne Publishers, 1991). An excellent examination of many different aspects and interpretations of García Márquez's multifarious masterpiece. Many imaginative flourishes, from chapters such as "An Imaginary Garden with Real Toads" to an authentic Sanskrit rendering of the crucial opening lines of Melquiades's poem that unlock for Aureliano the key to their meaning.

The Fragrance of Guava: Conversations Between Gabriel García Márquez and Plinio Apuleyo Mendoza (Faber and Faber, 1998). A series of conversations between García Márquez and his longtime friend, ranging over all manner of topics, from books to women.

Bernard McGuirk and Richard Cardwell, eds., *Gabriel García Márquez: New Readings* (Cambridge University Press, 1987). A range of perceptive essays on García Márquez's major works by a number of different authors. An added bonus comes in the form of a reprint of García Márquez's complete Nobel Prize speech.

Michael Wood, *Gabriel García Márquez: One Hundred Years of Solitude* (Cambridge University Press, 1990). Criticism with profound understanding and empathy, including many helpful explanations. For example, García Márquez's own reason for his parsimonious use of dialogue "because it doesn't ring true in Spanish."

Index

A NOTE ON THE AUTHOR

Paul Strathern has lectured in philosophy and mathematics and now lives and writes in London. He is the author of the enormously successful series Philosophers in 90 Minutes. A Somerset Maugham Prize winner, he is also the author of books on history and travel, as well as five novels. His articles have appeared in a great many publications, including the *Observer* (London) and the *Irish Times*.

Paul Strathern's 90 Minutes series in philosophy, also published by Ivan R. Dee, includes individual books on Thomas Aquinas, Aristotle, St. Augustine, Berkeley, Confucius, Derrida, Descartes, Dewey, Foucault, Hegel, Heidegger, Hume, Kant, Kierkegaard, Leibniz, Locke, Machiavelli, Marx, J. S. Mill, Nietzsche, Plato, Rousseau, Bertrand Russell, Sartre, Schopenhauer, Socrates, Spinoza, and Wittgenstein.